WRITE BETTER RIGHT NOW

WRITE BETTER RIGHT NOW

*The Reluctant Writer's Guide
to Confident Communication
and Self-Assured Style*

MARY-KATE MACKEY

CAREER
PRESS

Wayne, NJ

WRITE BETTER RIGHT NOW
Edited by Patricia Kot
Typeset by PerfecType, Nashville, Tennessee
Cover design by Joanna Williams
Cover image by oly5/123rf
Printed in the U.S.A.

To order this title, please call toll-free 1-800-CAREER-1 (NJ and Canada: 201-848-0310) to order using VISA or MasterCard, or for further information on books from Career Press.

The Career Press, Inc.
12 Parish Drive
Wayne, NJ 07470
www.careerpress.com
www.newpagebooks.com

Library of Congress Cataloging-in-Publication Data
CIP Data Available Upon Request.

DEDICATION

*For Annie Rose—who always follows through
with determination and grace.*

ACKNOWLEDGMENTS

I thought writing this book would be a solitary journey. It didn't happen that way. My thanks to my husband, Lou, who listened to ideas flying by and spent mornings alone—even as we traveled together—so I could work on the book; my son, Jacques, who continues to make sure my computer never dies, and his wife, Hanh, who always believed in this book; John, my daughter's partner, who contributed his considerable photography skills; and my daughter, Annie Rose, who has cheered me on every step of the way.

My thanks go to my writing group, The Editorial Board—Rosemarie Ostler, Deanna Mather Larsen, Kelly O'Brien, and Sophia McDonald Bennett. Thanks to Scott Landfield, owner of Tsunami Books in Eugene, Oregon, where the Board meets each week. Thanks to everyone who let me interview you or gave me permission to use your stories—including Kathleen Brenzel, Randy Dotinga, Nick Bernard, and James Baggett.

Thanks to my agent, Steve Harris, CSG Literary Partners; and the helpful editors at Career Press.

And finally, thanks to my students over the years. I only hope I taught you half of what you taught me.

CONTENTS

EDIT | Section 3 | 133

INTRODUCTION

Hello there...

You've got writing questions. I've got writing answers. Let's see if they match.

If you've picked up this book, you probably see yourself as a non-writer. Or perhaps you're an untrained writer. Or maybe you're a procrastinating writer who only turns in work after an intense struggle. In other words, you're a reluctant writer.

Reluctant writers can use this book as a springboard to get ahead in any job, passion project, or side hustle that requires writing skills. Whether you're called upon to create blog posts, presentations, web content, press releases, speeches, or just a great email, this step-by-step manual will get you there.

This book is for you if:

- **You don't have a lot of time.**
  Your time is short. This book is short. I know there's a literal ton (or two) of big, important, and great writing books you could buy. (I've included a reading list at the back of this book for some solid suggestions.) But if you need to improve your writing *today*—without having to wade through a lot of information to get to what works for you—read this book first.

- **You need practical advice.**
  Write Better Right Now offers a clear-cut process that can work for any form of writing. Three sections follow the

natural writing progression: **THINK (Chapters 1-3)**,
STRUCTURE (Chapters 4-7), and **EDIT (Chapters 8-11)**.
Plus, the Bonus Chapter 12 explores the fastest way to write
better—by tag-team editing with someone else.

- **You have specific writing problems you need to solve.**
  This book is problem-driven. Each chapter opens with a
  common writing problem and then offers solutions to that
  particular difficulty. The chapters end with exercises you can
  repeat any time you're stuck.

I Hate to Write

I was leading a seminar on writing techniques for a group
of professionals—all with different job titles. I asked everyone
around the table to tell me what their goals were for this
workshop. Responses ranged from the general, "I want tips
on making my writing better," to the specific, "I want to know
how to tell which part of the story is the most important."

But one woman had more on her mind. She looked
all business—tasteful blue tailored shirt, carefully highlighted
hair, and beautifully manicured nails.

"I have to write to go forward in my career. I have to
write a lot," she said. "I hate it."

I asked her what part she particularly hated most, but
the whole process of getting ideas into words seemed over-
whelming. There was a certain feeling that life had handed
her something she didn't see coming, something she hadn't
planned on. And she was a competitive woman who needed
to be prepared.

Finally she nailed it. With some heat, she said, "I don't
have the benefit of a journalism school degree!"

Well, I hear you there. Most of us don't.

At the end of the six-hour workshop, she left with ideas that we both hoped would make the writing process less painful. Since then, I've thought a lot about her comment. Here's the deal: you don't need a degree to write well—you just need some basic tools and tips.

In *Write Better Right Now*, I share the same concepts I taught for 14 years at the University of Oregon's School of Journalism and Communication. Not that I equate reading this book with a journalism degree—I don't. But these are the practical tactics my students learned when they took my upper division writing class.

So here's to your continuing success, Ms. Need-to-Write-to-Get-Ahead. And to all those others who approach writing with a certain angst, this book's for you!

How to Use *Write Better Right Now*

Read Step-by-Step

The progression of *Write Better Right Now* allows you to explore the big-picture writing process from beginning to end. If you have an orderly learning style, reading the book from start to finish might work well. But that's not the only way to use this book.

Jump in the Middle

Many people don't want, or need, the big picture, so don't read any more of this book than you have to. Each chapter of *Write Better Right Now* focuses on a specific writing problem. That way, as you meet different challenges, you can skip around the book to find the tools you need— right when you need them. You'll guide yourself to the next step.

Read Backward

If you're struggling with your writing at any point—back up. The cause of your problem lies in one of the steps behind you.

I heard this idea from Jack Hart, Pulitzer-winning editor and author of *The Writer's Coach* and *Storycraft*. It's so profound and simple, I've never forgotten it.

For example, let's say you have a terrible time editing your writing. You can't figure out what to keep and what to cut. Turn around and back up to the previous section on how to structure your writing. Use the information and exercises to clarify the structure you've chosen. After that, it will be much easier to see what doesn't fit when you edit.

Or maybe you have trouble when you start to write: you can't decide how to begin. Don't keep slogging in aimless circles. Back up to the preceding step—the thinking process. Re-examine basic questions like *Who am I writing this for? What's the point? What problem am I solving?* Those responses will help you launch your writing.

Do It Your Way

What's your learning style? This book gives you different ways to pick up the information you need. If you like straightforward advice, read the how-to's. If you learn by example, there are plenty to choose from. And if you like narratives, I've tucked in sidebar stories about real people tackling real writing problems.

But—there's always a *but*, isn't there?—it's not enough to read about writing. I encourage you to do the Write On exercises. They're as short, sharp, and useful as I can make them. They won't all work for you, but try them out to discover which ones are keepers.

Any way you do it, you can take small steps today that will make writing more satisfying and less of a hassle. The goal of this book is to move you out of the self-identified category of reluctant writer. You'll walk away with the skills and confidence to meet the challenge—when you have to write better right now.

THINK

SECTION 1 INTRODUCTION

"Writing is hard and bad for the health." That's how E. B. White summed up his experience—and lot of people would agree with him one hundred percent.

However, I don't think it's the *writing* that's so difficult—it's the *thinking*. This unseen work is the most overlooked—and toughest—part. Many of us assume that real writers sit down to write and creativity just erupts out of their brains, a light bulb flashing above their heads. And if that doesn't happen for us? Well, we conclude, we're just bad at writing. We go ahead and bang the words out, because it's required for whatever reason. The results are often flat, or unfocused, or just not very good. Worse, we don't know how to make it better. Now that's painful.

The truth? Good writing is not an act of genius. (Great writing, perhaps, but we're not going there.) However, not many of us have been taught the series of thinking steps that ultimately make the writing process smoother.

Okay, I know—I'm asking you to add more steps to something you already dislike. That may seem like way more work. But these tools will speed things up because they solve problems long before they even show up in your writing.

Think This Way

Thinking about writing takes two forms—cruise-along thinking and hard thinking. Cruise-along thinking is what we do 95 percent of the time. You're aware, you're processing, and you may even be making decisions. It's fairly easy.

But that last 5 percent? That effort requires real focus. That's hard thinking. And hard thinking, I believe, should be done for the shortest amount of time possible. We should reserve that exhausting work for a specific moment and then go all out. After all, anyone can handle hard work if you know it won't last forever. And as long as you buckle down for a few minutes at some point during the writing process, you can relax and cruise along for the rest of the time.

When Should You Do Hard Thinking?

To figure out when you should do heavy-duty thinking, it helps to identify your own natural writing method. Don Fry—veteran independent writing coach and author of *Writing Your Way: Creating a Writing Process That Works for You* and seventeen other terrific books—names two ways you might go about it: you could be a planner or a plunger. I'm adding a third way: you could be a matcher.

Are you a planner?

Planners often create a rough structure or swift outline before they launch into writing. It gives them a chance to see where they're going. This kind of organization is good for short pieces and great for longer or more complicated projects. If planning ahead is your style, you'll be doing your all-out thinking *before* you begin to write your draft.

Are you a plunger?

Plungers are those who have to actually write down their thoughts in order to find out what they're thinking. This works well for shorter pieces like essays, narratives, opinion pieces, and even emails—just don't hit "Send" automatically. Leaping directly into writing sometimes takes longer, but it's not a bad way to go. I often advocate jumping off the cliff (metaphorically, please) and trusting that you'll figure out what you're doing on the way down. But, after your first plunge into the writing sea, you still have to come out, dry off, and do your important mental heavy lifting *after* you write a first draft.

Or are you a matcher?

Perhaps you're someone who does a bit of both. You plan with a loose sketched-out series of ideas, plunge into writing for a while, and then go back to see if what you wrote resembles what you thought you wanted to get down. This approach can work for all kinds of writing. For matchers, you'll do your intensive thinking at the *in-between* point—whenever you're comparing your idea with your draft.

How the THINK Section Can Help

The clearer your thinking, the easier it is to get your ideas onto the page. In Chapter 1, you'll jumpstart your writing by answering **three questions** about who, what, and how. Chapter 2 lets you in on the best-kept secret for quick thinking: **copying**. And Chapter 3 shows you how to create a **cable-car sentence** that helps you find your focus fast.

With the THINK section's system of questions, tips, cheat sheets, and exercises, you'll be able to think—and then write—with the least possible agony.

CHAPTER 1

Get to the Point

Writing Problem: *I don't know where to start!*

Rx: *Answer three questions about people, problems, and promise.*

Beginning to write can be a stumper. There's a gap between what's in your head and what you want on the page. You experience that blank-screen moment. Or your fingers are moving madly and your brain is in the next room.

So let's prepare. Let's back up from writing and answer a few questions. It doesn't matter if the answers are rough or messy. The questions are the first step for getting the ideas from your head into the physical world. That's the only place you can actually work with them, mold them, cut them, and shape the thoughts like bread dough. Answer these **three main questions** (and a few minor ones) and you are well on your way.

The **Write On Exercise: Think Fast!** can be used for this beginning step whenever you start a new piece of writing. This chapter also has two **Words to the Wise** sections: **Play the Tone Scale** will help you determine how to approach your reader—from friendly to formal—and **What's My**

WIIFM? helps you judge the strength of your connection to your reader. **Real-World Review: Flip Your Thinking** features documentation writer Kelly O'Brien. Through her work, she shows the thinking process in action.

Question One: Who Cares?

Focus on People

Right now, forget about what you have to write. Forget about your ideas or your assignment. That's a relief, isn't it? Now let's look at something more concrete and easier to consider—your reader.

Ask yourself, who needs this? The answer is usually obvious—for example, you need to write a blog post for your customers. Or you might be writing a project proposal for a group at work, or an essay for a college admissions rep, or a cover letter to a job recruiter—you get the idea.

Write down the name of this person. If you imagine that person, your subsequent writing will be more specific. Depending on who they are, you might know them extremely well or not at all. But if you're addressing a group, name one person in it who could represent the whole—it's easier to write with one person in mind than to a crowd. If you don't know the person's name, make one up you like.

Think about your relationship. This could be your boss, a social media fan, a colleague, or a person you need to direct. Sometimes, you can't name a relationship. If you're at a complete loss, imagine someone friendly you'd like to talk to—not someone harsh and judgmental.

This is exactly what many marketing departments do when they are selling the company's product. They create a customer. They give their imaginary person a name—Sienna—and a title in a fake company—customer service manager, EnviroWorks—and they envision how Sienna would use their product. Sienna might even have a Twitter account, personal characteristics, and whole stories invented about how she handles problems. It's called "world building." While you don't need anything so elaborate, you might as well borrow this technique when you can't put a name to your reader.

By looking at names and relationships, your writing will hit the right tone (see Words to the Wise: Play the Tone Scale). Decide on these specifics up front and you'll also help yourself answer the next two questions.

Words to the Wise: Play the Tone Scale

When we communicate in person, we automatically adjust our tone. You talk in a different way to your brother, your boss, your five-year-old niece, or your bar buddy. The same is true with your writing—it's just that we don't usually categorize it. So, when you figure out your relationship to your reader, then you're empowered to make those same tone modifications in your writing.

To do that, think of these adjustments as occurring along a writing tone scale. One side would be formal or academic. Slide down to the other end and you'd find shortcuts, abbreviations, and colloquial slang.

- **Formal:** *Strict adherence to roadway traverse must be observed at all times.*
- **Informal:** *Stay on the path, dude.*

Formal	Informal
Academic	Conversational
Impersonal	Personal
Serious	Funny
Elaborate	Simple
Controlled	Unconventional

By naming your reader and what relationship they have with you, you'll locate your writing along this scale. Identifying the tone tells you a huge amount about *how* you will write something. The tone scale dictates word choices, verbs, sentence length, and all sorts of other picky details. Discovering the tone strengthens your voice—your distinctive manner of expression—and you haven't even started writing.

For example, you'd deliver a short reminder to your boss with brief sentences and specific verbs in a no-nonsense tone:

Your noon meeting is in the Webb Building. The discussion is on the liability of the roadway repair. A ten-minute Q&A will follow.

You might explain a cookie recipe with details that help readers understand the information, using a tone of friendly, but confident, authority:

This simple sand tart recipe makes a super-thin cookie, but it's not a tart and it isn't sandy. Handle as you would pie dough—as little as possible.

Or you'd employ casual language to send a warm invitation for readers to follow your blog:

My blog features the latest in environmental and animal news from around the globe. Follow along and share your own stories from the critter kingdom!

Question Two: What's the Difficulty?

Look at the Problem

Much of our written communication is about solving readers' problems. Problems can be all over the map, from simple to complex. For example:

- **Simple**—This person needs to know the conference schedule.
- **Complicated**—This person needs information about hospital statistics in order to persuade the administration to change protocol.

In any case, you solve readers' challenges with your writing.

Here's where you can do more world building. Allow your empathetic imagination to step in. Jot down details about the difficulties your reader is facing. The more you can add, the more chance you'll refine your focus. And that makes your future writing task easier.

Often the problem is that the reader lacks information. You supply it. Be specific about what's needed. Sometimes it helps to identify the problem and then ask questions about it. For example, let's say you need to write a piece for a farming newsletter. It's aimed at people interested in raising alpacas. You identify the problem—*Readers don't know what to consider when raising alpacas for wool.* After you nail the problem, you might write out questions like this:

> *Does diet matter? Does the type of soil on which alpacas are raised make a difference? Do bloodlines count for wool quality? Does weather affect the wool?*

If you know the answers to the questions—or can ask the people who do—you now have the information you need to build your piece.

Here's another example. Let's imagine there's been a shakeup in the nonprofit organization where you work. The leader who carried the ball has left. You've been assigned to give a presentation to the remaining board members about how to create an action plan for the future. But first, you need to figure out what's the board's problem. Turns out, this board has been rubber-stamping, allowing the departed leader to make all the decisions. So the problem? *The board members don't know how to take an active role.* Now you can research these questions:

> *What type of board do we have? What are the legal requirements? What are the specific duties?*

Your presentation is shaped before you've even written your first draft.

When writing a letter of complaint or a demand, the problem appears to lie with you and not the reader—*These supplies have not come in.* But think again in terms of the reader's problem. Perhaps they are unaware of the snafu. Or if they are aware, they have a problem because *your company is going to look elsewhere* for the supplies. Your clear writing gets them in the picture.

Sometimes writing situations don't seem to include problems. For example, do readers of college application essays have a problem? Start by imagining that essay reader—let's give her the name of Althea Perez. See her sitting there in her office? A stack of papers rises in front of her. All day long she's perusing what students write. What's her problem? *She needs to find potential students.* The application essay is one of the only ways she can judge. And she reads a lot of lousy essays. What does she need? Althea's looking for an essay that makes it easy for her to say yes. She'd like one that grabs her attention and gives her confidence that the student is ready for college.

Once you name her predicament, your marching orders become clearer. And oddly, even though you may be writing a personal essay, the task becomes less about you and more about solving the puzzle that will focus your writing. (Check out Chapter 7 for tips to create the personal essay that will make Althea say yes.)

Question Three: How Will My Writing Solve This Problem?

Picture the answer to this question in Hollywood lights. This is the vital connection between you—the writer—and your reader. Solving your reader's problem is at the very heart of your thinking process.

Now—and only now—should you return to your original writing idea or assignment. To match up your idea with the reader's problem, ask yourself, *What am I giving my reader that they don't have now?*

When you think in terms of results, you're making a promise to the readers. In the alpaca example above, would-be farmers get the information they need to make a decision. That's the promise. Or in the second example the presentation promises the board members that they will function more effectively after attending the presentation. For the slow supplier, your clear statement of the issue will get results one way or the other. If you can hook in that college essay reader with a snappy opening, your promise of a good read solves her recruiting problem.

Think of your problem solving as the quiet harbor with the readers out there bobbing on a sea of words. The promise becomes the lighthouse beacon that brings readers in. They spot what they need. They home in on you. They engage with what you have to say.

Problem-Solve for a Strong Promise

If you can't easily answer the question—*What am I giving my readers they don't have now?*—back up and look at your problem.

It might not be specific enough. You need to give the problem more focus. One way to sharpen is to imagine how you'd put the dilemma in the subject line of an email. Even if you're not writing an email, by paring down your problem to a bold eye-catcher, you'll know what to put in when you write (and what to leave out).

You might go back to your problem step and discover that you've got more than one difficulty to solve. In this case, you'll need to decide which is the most important point. If, as you write, you discover that another problem and its accompanying promise seem more important, you can always go back and change your emphasis.

Promises With Benefits

Most promises contain at least one of these three benefits. Readers will

- Gain knowledge or **information**.
- Enjoy the writing as **entertainment**.
- Be persuaded or moved to **action**.

Pick up any consumer magazine and you'll see this benefits pattern—often all three types are offered at once. For example, in a *New York Times Magazine* article, "The Wolf Hunters of Wall Street" (3/21/14), Michael Lewis gives us an exposé about stock market players getting cheated by high-speed trading. The promise is a grabber with three benefits—*you'll gain insider knowledge about high-speed trades* (**information**), *you'll be taken to a mind-blowing world you know nothing about* (**entertainment**), and *you'll come away wanting to change the laws so everything is more transparent* (**action**).

Check out a few more examples of how these work.

For a nonprofit's donor ask-letter:

Your profile on a cooking school for at-risk youth shows one participant turning her life around and opening her own food truck.

- **People:** Nonprofit donors
- **Problem:** Donors don't know how their money is used.
- **Promise:** You'll understand how important your contributions are (**information**) in this engaging story (**entertainment**) and be motivated to give again (**action**).

For a food suppliers' trade newsletter:
Your review of seven money-saving shortcuts using the latest apps.

- **People:** Food suppliers
- **Problem:** Food suppliers have tight margins and need to save money.
- **Promise:** Read this and you'll up your profits (**information**).

For a status report:
Your analysis of the results of a survey.

- **People:** Your boss
- **Problem:** Company is confronting customers' changing buying habits.
- **Promise:** Read this (**information**) and make a move based on the data (**action**).

But what if you need to address two or more people at the same time and each has different requirements? To avoid confusion or a lack of focus, use the people/problem/promise for each person. Once you're clear on that, you can figure out how to structure your writing so that all needs are met.

In this example, suppose you're a program manager sending a short email about an upcoming project to two people. You're emailing both your supervisor, Cheryl (who needs a big picture update), and your department assistant, Sean (who needs a specific task assignment). Sort out who needs what problem solved before you write and your task becomes quicker and your writing sharper.

Hi Cheryl and Sean,

*The web migration project will start the week of June 14. Our goal is to have the new site live by the end of August. Cheryl, you'll receive weekly updates from me on progress or any roadblocks. (**big picture**)*

Sean, to kickoff this project, please: **(specific task)**

- *Schedule a meeting with all project stakeholders for early next week to review the plan*
- *Finalize the current sitemap*
- *Confirm pricing options with our vendor*

Thanks,

Zelda

As you get comfortable with converting your thinking into problem-solving mode, you may find yourself jumping straight to the question of, "How does my idea solve the reader's problem?" That's great, as long as your answer is short and specific. If not, back up to the steps before and consider who this person is and what they need.

Think Now—Write Later

Thinking is the most underrated part of writing. By taking the time to familiarize yourself with these tools—I promise, it takes longer to read this chapter than to actually answer the questions—you'll lay the foundation for your writing construction. If you define the specifics first, your whole writing job ahead gets easier.

Words to the Wise: What's My WIIFM?

Another way to make sure your writing is focused on your reader's needs is to rank your piece on the WIIFM scale.

WIIFM is the acronym for the question every reader wants to know: **W**hat's **I**n **I**t **F**or **M**e?

Sometimes, your writing project is so short and clear you can skip this question. But if your writing is complicated, your idea unclear, or you just want another way to think about the whole thing, try giving your concept a WIIFM rank—high, medium, or low.

High WIIFMs

If your idea closely matches the needs of your reader, that's a high WIIFM. For example:

- *An article for an orchid newsletter—Gives orchid fanatics the information from the experts on how to keep their plants healthy.*
- *A report to boss—Shows that your small business has added a hundred additional service contracts and delineates where they came from.*
- *A blog post for Allaboutbirds.com—Tells cockatiel owners five signs that their birds are at death's door and what to do about it.*

Low WIIFMs

If there's a gap between your idea and the needs of your reader, that would score a low WIIFM ranking. For example:

- *A memo on information about customer preferences— You put in production numbers instead.*
- *An annual report—Needs the metrics for institutional effectiveness, but you included the history of the institution.*
- *A letter to past donors about a river restoration— Features details so complex the donors see no practical application for their money.*

If you've identified a strong WIIFM, great! Move on! But if you think your WIIFM might be low, back up a step and check out how you identified your reader's problem. Ask yourself again, "How will my idea solve the reader's problem?" That's the basis for engagement.

Sometimes you have to reshape the idea to raise the WIIFM. You can sharpen it with more information. Sometimes the needs can be targeted with more focus and less extraneous information. The higher the WIIFM, the stronger the communication.

Write On Exercise: Think Fast!

Time: Five minutes, max

The exercises in this book can be used any time you're faced with a writing task. I've suggested time limits to help keep your answers quick and your efforts to a minimum. Find a timer that counts down in seconds. This will measure how long you will free-write.

Timed writing makes heavy-lifting thinking easier. For a free-write you begin writing as the timer starts and don't stop until the timer stops—not for a moment. Try to respond to the question, but don't judge. Allow the words to come. Your job is to catch them as they go by. No grammar rules. No need for complete sentences. You can type or write by hand. Sometimes it's fun to mix it up; hand write if you usually type. Ideas may appear differently depending on how they're executed. Experiment. The point is to let whatever is there come out. Even if it's just, "shit, shit, shit..." keep on going. Trust that you'll get bored and move on to other words.

Step 1. Answer three questions.

- **People: Who's this for?** (15 seconds) Guess, if you don't know exact details.
- **Problem: What's my reader's problem?** (45 seconds) Be as specific as you can. If you have time, add more details.
- **Promise: How does my good idea solve the problem?** (30 seconds)

Figure out what's your promise. Try as many wordings as you can fit into the time.

Step 2. Review. When you have finished, whether you're working alone or with others (see Chapter 12), read what you've written. Pick out words or phrases that seem most important.

Find the answers to these questions, and you can use them as you move forward. Then, rank your WIIFM. If it's high, move on. If low, repeat the exercise for more specifics.

Real-World Review: Flip Your Thinking

*Documentation writer Kelly O'Brien tells how
focusing on the reader solves problems.*

"My job is to translate developer-speak into normal English." That's the way Kelly describes her freelance work for a variety of clients, most of them software or web development companies. This Ithaca College journalism grad turns technical information about her clients' sites or products into more widely accessible user manuals.

It's vital. Picture a chasm—like the Grand Canyon—with the developers gathered on the North Rim and the users waiting on the South. Documentation writers must create a bridge that spans that chasm, connecting the features that developers create with the benefits users need.

"Developers get very excited about what the product does," Kelly says. "They know all about what they have made, the elegant fixes. But users don't care how it works. They only get excited if it helps them get their jobs done."

Kelly starts her bridge building on the users' side of the canyon. Instead of writing about the wonderful features, she says, she becomes a user. "I play with the tool so I know how it works. If it doesn't do what I expect it to do, I dig down until I really know what's going on."

She returns to the developers if she needs more information. "My narrative sense of storytelling helps me pin down the areas where developers' communication is fuzzy. Trying to tell a coherent story about how a product works makes it easier to see holes."

Even though her topic is the product, she flips her thinking around and focuses on the problems a user might have. And not just an imaginary user. "Her name is Doris," Kelly says. "She's a real person."

Years before, Kelly worked with Doris at a university research center. Doris was using Filemaker, a relational database program. "But she was not using it consistently," Kelly notes. "To make her job easier—and our records more coherent—I documented the steps of common tasks for her."

Now, whenever Kelly picks up a new documentation project, she sees Doris as her target audience. "I imagine the places where she would get frustrated. Where it's complicated, I'll make the tone extra friendly and keep the steps very simple and clear. In the easy parts, I'll cut down the commentary and just walk her through."

And in the end, all that upside-down thinking results in products that can be used with ease. "I love that I'm creating intuitive content that describes a not-so-intuitive tool," she says. "I get to Rubik's Cube the writing—every piece coming at you where it needs to be."

CHAPTER 2

Copy, Copy, Copy

Writing Problem: *I don't know how to write what I have to write.*

Rx: *Copy first, create later.*

Over the years, many reluctant writers have confided in me some variation on the statement, "I'm a terrible writer." They know that their written communication is messy, unclear, and unorganized. But they don't see any way out. Yet many of these same people can produce a meal from a cookbook, or follow a knitting pattern, or navigate a strange city using step-by-step driving instructions. If they had a recipe for writing, they could follow it as well.

That's where copying comes in.

In this chapter, you'll see how copying lets you to get into the shoes of another writer and deconstruct the format. Once you find the pattern, you can create your own formula, structure, and recipe. It's a down and dirty shortcut to make writing easier.

Put yourself in a copying frame of mind with **Words to the Wise: Get Judgmental**. The **Cheat Sheet: Deconstruction 101** contains all the questions you need to ask to make copying work for you. Plus, the **Write**

On Exercise: Deconstruct Anything helps you figure out writing patterns. Finally, **Real-World Review: Copy for Success** explains how one beginning writer was taught the ropes by a person who didn't exist.

Why Copy?

In our culture, copying gets a bad rap. From the moment a first-grader hollers, "Teacher, he's copying me!" everyone knows copying is a terrible thing to do. As a society, we value the unique, not the derivative.

And yet, it all depends on how and what you copy. Copying can be the quickest way to teach yourself what you need to know. I'm not talking about stealing answers to test questions or plagiarizing someone else's words. I'm talking about deconstruction.

Here's the basic idea: Find a piece of writing you like, or that fits your needs, and then take it apart, line by line. Figure out how it works. Whether it's a snappy email, detailed report, or informative newsletter, if you understand the pieces, you can follow the format. After you decipher the pattern, you can plug in your own ideas and subjects.

If you've wandered by paintings in a museum, you've probably seen copying in action. In art education, it's a time-honored tradition for students to set up their easels and learn by imitating the masters.

So why not do the same with writing?

On the Example Hunt

The first step is to find writing models you can copy. If you're writing on the job, the examples may include work created by your colleagues. If you have nothing to guide you within your company, go further afield to find writing you admire or would like to copy.

Sometimes, the examples you have to work with are dense and packed with information. Don't let this discourage you. Complexity is not a crime. If you're looking at detailed pieces—especially in the academic or deeply theoretical world—you can still take the writing apart. You just need to attack it at a slower pace. Move through, noting exactly what information is loaded into those sentences. All writers have patterns. It's your job to find out what they are.

Now, these examples don't have to be the world's most perfect writing. Instead, focus on what interests you. Look for writing that you can relate to. Even if you think you don't know enough about writing to have an opinion, go with your gut feeling. (See Words to the Wise: Get Judgmental for more ideas on how to conquer this anxiety.)

You can also ask for other people's recommendations. It doesn't matter if they like different writing than you do. Discovering why someone admires a certain kind of writing is always illuminating, especially if you haven't noticed it before.

The next step is to figure out *why* the piece is interesting. Does it solve a problem? Does it make your job (or another's) easier? Is it full of facts you find fascinating or useful? The answers to these questions become the clues to improve your own written communication.

Words to the Wise: Get Judgmental

As a reluctant writer, you may feel really uncomfortable when you start the hunt for writing you can copy—how do you even know what's good? But if you read at all, you do actually judge writing on a daily basis. And you can develop your own perspective by noticing what interests you and what doesn't.

At first, you don't have to focus on the kind of writing you need to do—you're simply trying to focus on what appeals to you and why it attracts you. Is it a graphic novel? A magazine article? A social media rant?

If you can, take notes. For three days, jot down whatever calls to you. What draws you in? Why does it? And conversely, what bores the crap out of you? What do you dismiss? After three days, you may see your own pattern of preference. By examining what you like and why you like it, you'll start to trust and develop your own discernment.

Find the Framework

Now that you have examples, let's look at *how* they're constructed. Here are six steps to take apart a piece of writing and look at the mechanics that make it tick.

1. The Opening

How does it begin? The best start, no matter what kind of writing, tells the reader something about what will follow. If it's an email, what does the subject line look like? Is it clear what it's about? Or if it's a report, does the writing open with a series of compelling facts that make the reader want to know how they were achieved? Perhaps it makes a sweeping statement or offers an opinionated point of view. If it's a profile, does it start with a quote that tells you where the writing is headed? Here's a compelling start to a business profile:

> **Example:** *It's ironic that just after I launched my new line of bras, I was diagnosed with breast cancer and ended up with a double mastectomy.*

Now that's a statement that makes a reader want to find out how the business got launched in spite of the challenges, and of course, to discover how the owner's health is now.

Copy it: If you were copying that business profile, you could also start with a summation quote from the person you are writing about—probably nothing to do with health, but some other challenge—that would hook the reader and focus the story. You'd hunt through your notes to see if you had one. If you didn't, you'd go back and ask the question that will get you what you need. (See Chapter 5 for more ideas on the art of the interview.)

2. Word Count

This is so basic it's often overlooked. When you're imitating, it's good to replicate the same number of words. An approximation of the word count helps determine the scope of your writing.

Example: If you have a digital copy, you can easily get a word count. But here's a trick for any print paper copy. Assume, give or take, that the top digit of your thumb is an inch. Count the words in a thumb's inch of copy, and measure down the rest of the piece, one thumb length at a time. Then multiply that number by the number of words in the first inch. That gives you an approximation of how many words are in the copy. Obviously, if the margins change—say, around a photo—you'll have to recount another inch in that new place and then measure on for the new width. I counted this paragraph out using the thumb method—135 words—and then checked with the computer—129. Close enough for copying.

Copy it: It's really about fitting your ideas into the length you're copying. Huge concepts cannot be compressed into 400 words. If what you're copying is short, and what you have to say is long, you'd need to zero in on a single chunk for your focus. On the other hand, knowing the word count on longer pieces allows you to build and go into more detail.

3. Titles, Subtitles, and Subheads

Titles, subtitles, and subheads all allow readers to skim over material without having to read every word. That can be a good thing for busy people. These three also function as entry points to engage the reader. Almost all writing has a title, but check whether the piece you're imitating uses subtitles—the words after the main title—or subheads—those short phrases or sentences that break up articles into sections. Look at how all three—if you have them—are conveying information. How frequently do they appear? In a blog post, every short section may have a subhead. In a more in-depth piece, they might appear once every 300 words. Here's the breakdown of a blog post for a career website.

Example:

Title: *Four Things You Must Know About Finding a Career You Love*

Subtitle: *Finding your passion isn't all it's cracked up to be. Here's what you should know before pursuing yours.*

Subheads:

- *Passion Is Created, Not Discovered*
- *Take Action (aka Stop Thinking)*
- *Focus on Lifestyle Issues*
- *Your Passions (Can) Change*

Copy it: If you were copying this example with a different subject, you would see that the title says this is a numbers article. The subtitle turns an assumed idea (everyone must have a passion to be happy) upside down.

It also uses two sentences. And the four subheads give information about concrete steps for readers to take. That's a pattern you can follow.

4. Paragraphs

Notice how the writing you're copying handles paragraphs. Are they long or short? Are there any single-sentence paragraphs? Email paragraphs tend to be a few sentences because they're easier read in one sweep of the box. Blog posts also lean toward shorter paragraphs for readability on devices. Other kinds of writing allow for more sentences in each paragraph, perhaps as many as six or eight.

How many paragraphs are there altogether? The count is simple in something short. If you need to copy something longer, look at a page and notice how many paragraphs fill it.

Example: Turn to page 45 in this chapter and look over the story "Copy for Success." The piece contains 13 paragraphs. The first three average five sentences each, of varying lengths. The next eight paragraphs are much shorter. At the end, two single-sentence paragraphs make the writing casual and immediate.

Copy it: Using this general format, you could now write your own essay about another subject. You'd put in about the same number of paragraphs. You'd construct sentences with a variety of word counts to match the example. As the story builds, you'd shorten the paragraphs. Using this pattern for your own thinking is mechanical, but it works.

5. Signpost Sentences

In most writing, paragraphs kick off with a sentence that's like a signpost, pointing readers in the right direction. (Chapter 10 has an in-depth look at signpost sentences.) Sometimes, in looser writing styles, the signpost appears further down into the paragraph. It's not as traditional, but if the communication is clear, it works. And you can copy it.

Let's do a quick overview of how signposts can work for you.

In the writing example you're working with, skim through the piece, reading only the signposts. Do you understand where the writing is headed?

Example: Let's imagine these are the first sentences of six paragraphs in a blog post about coworking spaces.

1. *"Welcome to the Hobbit Hole," she said.* What follows is a description of a building with coworking office spaces that can be rented by the hour, the day, or the month.
2. *Shared coworking spaces are becoming more popular by the month.* This paragraph describes the trend and the benefits— including the idea that freelancers and startup workers are the primary users.
3. *But is coworking all it's cracked up to be?* Now the writing asks question about the assumption. The writer provides a counter-argument that more traditional workspaces can actually lead to more productivity.
4. *Regardless, all signs point to the idea that coworking spaces aren't going away anytime soon.* The observation here focuses on the growing investment and development to create more shared working space across the United States.
5. *Look out for those Hobbit Holes.* The last paragraphs highlight the idea that coworking spaces signal a shift in corporate America that can't be overlooked.

Copy it: The signpost sentences you create can do the same. You could describe a trend, then project an assumption about it, turn that on its head, and end with a cautionary note on how to observe that trend. With signposts, you create an outline of thought.

6. Word Choice

Verbs set the tone of a piece more than anything else, so the easiest way to copy a style is to study the verbs. Go through and highlight every verb you can find. Are there lots of *to be* verbs like *is*, *are*, and *were?* Or do you find livelier examples?

How many syllables in the verbs also says a lot. Are there snappy one-syllable verbs, like *plunge, kick, tweak, raid,* and *sweep?* Or three- or more syllable verbs like *rectify, attenuate, elucidate, incentivize, incapacitate,* and *anthropomorphize?* They set the tone.

You can also look for whether certain words are repeated, how acronyms are handled, or if industry-specific jargon is used. Nothing's wrong with these communication shortcuts as long as your intended reader will understand.

Example: From a car gadget review: *The latest advance in technological wizardry is a wide-angle video for your car. This has been done before on a dashboard screen, but now it has been moved to where it should be—on the rear-view mirror itself.*

Copy it: For your review, you could rely on those short *to be* and single-syllable verbs.

Example: On the other hand, you could find something like this: *Recent studies conducted by data scientists indicate that people determine their preferences only after consulting with others.*

Copy it: Notice how many three-syllable verbs and other long words show up. Time to utilize your thesaurus.

7. The Ending

In your writing example, how does it end? If it's something as simple as an email, how does this person sign off? Is it appropriate for you to do the same? Or is there a hierarchy where your manager signs one way, and you another? Perhaps a story has been told, and the piece ends with the reason for the narrative. Maybe a call to action is given. Or you find a summation, or a reference back to the beginning. Sometimes the writing starts with the most relevant information and ends with the least important details. Any way you find it, you can copy.

Example: *In the end, it's important to remember the people who work there are a company's most important asset. It's not about data mining. It's not about strategic planning. It's certainly not about how smart management is. A company runs when its workers run with it.*

Copy it: This is a strong summation of the ideas. You ask the reader to remember your point. You say what it's not in a series of rhythmic sentences and finish with a strong image.

There's no right or wrong way here. You're hunting down the clues that will tell you how to structure your own writing in the same communication style.

Cheat Sheet: Deconstruction 101

Kick off your copying by asking these deconstruction questions. Once you know the answers, copy using your own ideas and words. It's a fast way to get your writing on track.

1. **Opening**
   - How is the first sentence constructed?
   - How many sentences in the first paragraph?
2. **Word Count and Length**
   - How many words are in the whole piece?
   - On average, how many words are in each paragraph?
   - How many paragraphs are in the piece?
3. **Titles, Subtitles, and Subheads**
   - Does the piece have a title?
   - Does it have a subtitle? How about subheads?
   - How long or short are any of these?
4. **Paragraphs**
   - Are they long or short?
   - How many paragraphs are there?
5. **Signpost Sentences**
   - Are the signpost sentences located at the beginning of the paragraph?
   - Do they follow in a logical sequence?
6. **Word Choice**
   - Are verbs active or are there many *to be* verbs?
   - Are the verbs complex (with three or more syllables, like *elucidate*)? Or snappy (like *point, rush, jog*)?
   - Does the piece contain jargon, acronyms, or words specific to a certain field, industry, or interest group?

7. **Ending**
- How is the last paragraph constructed?
- How many sentences does it contain?
- How is the last sentence constructed?

Bad Writing Can Be Your Guide

Bad writing can be as revealing as good writing—especially if you figure out why it's bad. Instead of avoiding incomprehensible writing in your field, start a collection of the truly awful.

Once you get your hands on some terrible writing, the fun part begins. Try to figure out a fix. Any fix. Bad communication is a puzzle that can be solved many ways. Does the verb—actually finding it can sometimes be a challenge—leave the subject in the dust? What was the writer trying to say? Is there a better/cleaner/shorter way to do that?

Here's an example I've put together. Writing this way is a bit like purposely singing off-key. I've tried to connect an assortment of words that still makes sense.

In the present effort to make certain concepts and natural world relationships clear to others, and at the same time to convincingly demonstrate the relevance of these to human concerns of a fundamental and more general nature, I have had direct evidence—and not for the first time—that teaching about the intricate connections in the biology and geology around us and learning about the same are intimately intertwined; or stated more cogently, they are but the two sides of the same coin. Indeed, teaching is learning, or should be. In point of fact, and in all candor, I may as well admit that I have become increasingly aware that through this process, through these exertions, my perception of teaching's sensitivity to cultural determinants (and with respect to these, its capacity of reflection without distortion), as well as, and especially, my recognition of its potential for transcendence—all of these have been steadily and significantly enhanced.

Whew! That's communication shrouded in a cascade of words.

Could you get through it? Please note that the whole paragraph consists of three sentences, the first one ending in the word *coin*. For fun, go through a phrase or two and see how many words you could cut out. I think this person is saying, "You can learn a lot through teaching." What do you think?

Write On Exercise: Deconstruct Anything

Time: Fifteen minutes

With this exercise, you can practice the ins and outs of copying at its best.

Step 1. Find an example. This can be anything you want to take apart.

Step 2. Categorize it. Go through and decide what category each sentence falls into. Mark after each with one or more of the following letters:

Anecdotes/Scenes—**A**

Authorities/Sources—**S**

Facts/Descriptions—**F**

Quotes—**Q**

Tips—**T**

Writer's Opinion/Point of View/Summary/Conclusions—**W**

Step 3. Note the quantity of categories. See how many of which kind you have. If you find some that don't fit these categories, make up your own. There's no right or wrong here. You're looking for a pattern you can copy. Are there three facts, one tip, and five writer's conclusions? In what order are they presented? Does the piece start with an anecdote laced with quotes, and then end with facts to back up the assertions?

Let's say you need to write a description about a success story for your nonprofit company's newsletter. Here's how you might deconstruct it:

Last year, Julia A. stood in the middle of a dusty clinic in the rural outskirts of Quito, Ecuador. **(A) (F)** *She fiddled with one of the recycled hearing aids she'd brought with her from Seattle, Washington, working to get it to properly fit in a young woman's ear.* **(F)**

"She was pregnant and she was so excited to be getting the hearing aid—she'd never had one before," *Julia remembers. "Because now she'd be able to hear her new baby cry for the very first time."* **(Q)**

It was moments like these that made Julia's volunteer project all worth it... **(W)**

This writing contains a tiny scene set in Ecuador, two facts, one quote, and a summation/conclusion. If you needed to write in that style, you could copy the pattern for your own story.

Copying Connects a World of Words

We live in a sea of words. Writers use this sea, explore it, look under the surface, notice changes in the currents, and check out what lives there. Reluctant writers tend to ignore the sea. They sit on the shore, listen to the roar, bored or overwhelmed by the thought of entering in.

Copying allows you to blow up your own rubber raft and float along. You're not in the sea, but you're on it. Even if you do nothing else but remain on your raft, copying gets you out on the water. The more you copy, the more you'll notice the words around you. And the more familiar you are, the more command you take. Eventually, if you hang in there, you might flip over the side and immerse yourself. Welcome to another world.

Real-World Review: Copy for Success
When I started out, I took help wherever I could find it.

My writing career was launched by someone who doesn't exist. Years ago, I sat on an advisory board for my town's National Public Radio station. As usual, they needed funds. At a board meeting, I suggested we raise the extra $3,000 by running a garden tour, where homeowners would open their gardens for a day. The station engineer seemed genuinely confused: "Who would want to look at someone else's garden?"

Of course, the board saddled me with the job to write a brochure about the tour and the gardens. This brochure had to be so alluring, so descriptive, so compelling that the engineer's question would be blown out of the water. But how? I'd never written a brochure or anything else about gardens. I was overwhelmed. Then the White Flower Farms plant catalog arrived in the mail.

White Flower Farms has a spokesperson, Amos Pettingill. The front of the catalog features his yearly introduction of their wares. He writes in the folksy, warm, and enthusiastic tones of an educated New England farmer. His descriptions always make me want to buy every plant. Then and there, I decided to write my brochure in the style of Amos Pettingill.

So, how did he arouse my lust for all those plants? First of all, I noticed he never said *I* but used the royal *we*. Okay, for this brochure, *we* could do that.

Amos had a warm tone. We adopted one too. *Welcome to the KLCC Garden Tour.*

Amos liked his adjectives. We rounded up a few. *We are featuring two fabulous gardens in the River Road neighborhood and a walking tour of ten exceptional gardens around Monroe Park.*

He used effusive descriptions. So did we. *This is a pleasant neighborhood, full of fine mature trees, well-kept homes, and many avid gardeners. Interesting front yards abound on every street.*

Amos chose words like *breathtaking, love,* and *delight.* We straight up copied him. *Our breathtaking gardens come in all sizes and reasons. We'd love to inspire and delight you and make your day out truly pleasurable.*

There was always a gentle, directive tone. We tried for the same. *Please, only visit the gardens on the day of the tour, and only at the open hours. Be a good neighbor when it comes to parking by driveways or narrow roads. And remember, do not pick any plant materials or step into the planting beds.*

To encourage sales, the free brochures were handed out as advertising at ticket locations around the town. By the end of the tour day, the radio station had taken in $20,000, thanks in part to the guidance of Amos Pettingill.

Later, a more experienced garden writer told me Amos is not a real person. He falls in with fictional brand representatives like Uncle Ben, Betty Crocker, and the hard-working Colombian coffee farmer, Juan Valdez.

And I thought I knew him so well.

Nonetheless, we are honored to have walked in his highly successful footsteps.

CHAPTER 3

The Dreaded Theme Statement

Writing Problem: *My writing ideas are wandering and unfocused.*

Rx: *Create a cable-car sentence to take you where you want to go.*

"Theme statement."

Those two words can strike fear into the hearts of many reluctant writers. It's not your fault. Many of us were made to write theme statements at an early age, long before we had developed the ability to think in abstracts. Or we were given theme statements in the guise of "prompts" and asked to write on demand about concepts we'd never considered. Alternatively, if you never had to wrestle with theme statements, creating one might feel like walking into a dark cave without a flashlight.

But theme statements are still the most powerful guide for everything you write. So in this last chapter of the THINK section, we're going to give theme statements a makeover. First, we're going to picture them more vividly by renaming them. Second, we'll break down your writing ideas into a fill-in-the-blank sentence to propel you into your next steps.

Chapter 3 also has a useful **Cheat Sheet: Name That Category** and the **Write On Exercise: Two Minutes of Heavy Lifting** to shortcut your thought process. In the **Real-World Review: Two Minutes in Action**, I'll share my own scribbled notes about how the exercise shaped a magazine story.

Swap Out Theme Statements for Cable-Car Sentences

The term *theme statement* is not very descriptive. Such an important writing tool should activate your imagination. In place of *theme statement*, I work with two other terms that are more dynamic. Because the theme statement's job is to guide your thinking, I like to call it a *guide sentence*— at least it shows its function. I use it, and I hope you will too. But I prefer an even more graphic descriptor—the *cable-car sentence*. Here's why it can help your writing.

Think about what a cable car does. Picture yourself standing on a steep street in San Francisco. Is the cable car coming? If you want to know, all you need to do is stand near the tracks and listen. You can't see the cable, but you can hear it, zinging along underground, embedded in the roadway. When the car stops, you step on board. Inside, the gripman shifts a long lever that allows a mechanism to clamp onto that ever-moving metal hawser hidden below the tracks. The car is drawn up the hill, clanging its bell, with people getting on and off along the way.

Your guide sentence is like that cable car. You can pack your ideas on board—hang a few good ones on the outside of a messy first draft—and ride the car up the writing hill. Basically, it's a way to keep all your ideas headed in the same direction.

I like the image of a cable car for a couple reasons. First, I like the picture of a rising hill, because much good writing follows an upward arcing trajectory. (We'll look at that arc in more detail in Chapter 4.)

Second, I also like the ability of a cable car to climb the hill with a certain effortlessness. (If you want to take a leap into the fanciful here, you could say the ever-moving cable might be your own creativity—or the universe's creativity—zinging along unseen.) The important point is that the writing hill may be steep, but the content moves along.

The third neat thing about a visualizing a cable car is that the riders get on and off. This is helpful because when you're in the editing stage, a cable-car sentence tells you which ideas to keep, and which should get off at the next stop.

With a strong cable-car sentence to convey your thoughts, the time for both writing and editing gets shorter. So let's drop the vague (and often hated) *theme statement* and give cable-car imagery a chance to guide your writing where it needs to go.

How to Create a Cable-Car Sentence

Find your focus fast and define the essence of your writing by breaking your thoughts into this fill-in-the-blanks sentence:

In my _____ (writing category) about _____ (subject) I am saying that _____ (slant).

Let's look at the blanks.

Writing Category

It's important to know what kind of writing you're doing because it changes the way you write it. The category may be obvious—you probably know it's a blog, or a report, or a presentation. If nothing comes to mind, check the Cheat Sheet: Name That Category. Then, if nothing fits, insert the word *piece* and keep going. You may be able to fill that blank in later when you know more about what you're writing.

Subject

The subject is usually easy. People ask, "What are you writing about for the company newsletter?" You answer, "The new widget our department is rolling out." Okay. The subject is the new widget.

Slant

The slant is your premise or your main point. It's your take on the subject. The term *slant* is sometimes used to describe biased writing, but here I'm using *slant* as the focus of your piece. News reporters see the difference between subject and slant with these two questions: *What's the news? What's the story?* The *news* is that the road is closed. The *story* is all the information about how that happened.

For instance, for your department's new widget, the slant is what you have to say about it. If you don't already know your slant when you start the project, you can research it. Collect notes that will answer questions like *What does the widget do? Who needs it? Why do they need it? How does it compare to other widgets? How did it come into being? What's the future of this widget? What does it mean for this company?* The answer to any one of these questions could become the particular slant for this piece of writing.

The Shifting Slant

Your subject can stay the same, but depending on the category and what you have to say, the slant could alter. Let's look at three examples of cable-car sentences. Each one shows the widget's story in action.

> In my *blog post* (category) about the *new widget* (subject), I am
> saying that *the projected sales of this product will rocket the company
> to new heights of fame and fortune* (slant on future benefits).

Then all the other information—what it does, who needs it, the history of development, how does it compare—could support your main premise.

Or let's say you're told to chronicle the history of the widget's arrival in the company newsletter. Your guide sentence would read:

> In my *profile* (category has changed) about *the new widget* (same
> subject) I am saying that *its successful arrival hinged on the impor-
> tant contributions of (names here) in this department* (slant now on
> the people who developed it).

Then you'd tell the story from the widget's inception, move through to the triumphant rollout, and mention all those people and their contributions. You would still keep in other facts like what the widget does, who needs it, or the future projections, but now all those would support your story. They're not the main focus.

Or let's just say that for some reason—you're a disgruntled employee?—you decide to write an exposé (not for the newsletter) about the rollout of this widget. The subject stays the same. The supporting facts remain. But now you might grab quotes from folks who applaud the rollout and those who think it's a terrible idea. Your sentence might read:

> In my *exposé* (category) about *the newest widget* (subject), I am saying that *while bosses project the sales will rocket the company to new heights of fame and fortune, insiders think it will crash and burn* (slant is focused on tell-all prediction).

Notice that in all these slants, strong verbs carry the action—*rocket, hinged, project, agree,* and *crash and burn*. Any time you're writing a slant, try to put in the most active verbs.

Cheat Sheet: Name That Category

Nonfiction writing shows up in innumerable forms and formats. I've listed some of the most common.

Analysis	Memoir
Blog post	Newsletter
Biography	News report
Brochure	Obituary
Directive	Opinion/editorial
Direct mail	Pitch
Email	Profile
Essay	Public service announcement
Exposé	Question/answer
Feature article	Research results
How-to	Sales pitch
Interview	Speech
Letters	Social media post
Memo	Visual presentation

How to Figure Out Your Slant

Most times, the writing category and subject are straightforward. The slant is where many people get stuck. One way to find your slant is to ask yourself, *"What's the most important thing I need to communicate?"* The answer will give you your focus. For example:

> In my *email* about *using the new customer management system,* I am saying that *because of changes to functionality, you need to attend the training next week.*

You could give it more urgency by picturing your guide sentence as a headline on a magazine cover. You won't write the email like that, but it's another way to find focus.

> In my *email* about *using the new customer management system,* I am saying that—*attend the training to get all the insider info!*

Or think in terms of movie dramatics or humor.

> In my *email* about *using the new customer management system,* I am saying that—*attend the training and save the world!*

But sometimes, your subject is complex or your thoughts about the slant are running around in circles. Perhaps you've gathered so much information you can't figure out what your slant should be. That's when you can rely on one of the handiest thinking tools I know: Two Minutes of Heavy Lifting.

I first learned the basics of this free-write exercise from a presentation given by reporter, writer, and Poynter Institute coach Chip Scanlon at a News Train conference for journalism students. I have modified the questions and expanded the exercise so you can build your slant after you've pared your thinking down to a single word.

Write On Exercise: Two Minutes of Heavy Lifting

Time: Two minutes

I've experimented by writing these exercises on a computer and then another time by hand. You might get different results as to thoughts, length, or quality. Also, the method you prefer may not be the one that's most productive, so try out both. Keep going as fast as you can until the time's up.

Step 1. Set the timer. Answer the question and reset the timer for the next question.

1. What's this piece of writing about? (45 seconds)
2. Why is it being told? (30 seconds)
3. How does it connect to the greater world? (20 seconds)
4. What's the point? (15 seconds)
5. In one word, what's this about? (10 seconds)

Step 2. Study the single word. No matter what kind of writing you're going for, the single words usually have a big-picture quality about them. Words that have been shared in my workshops and classes reflect that: *balance, perspective, realignment, accountability, survival, perseverance, irony, passion, sacrifice, change, nostalgia, values, chaos, imagination, journey, passion, adoption, assimilation, black box.* These words often describe universal truths. These words connect you to your readers.

Step 3. Create your slant. Take that word and construct the slant for the cable-car sentence. If you had more than one word, try a sentence for each. You may find strong verbs that will help you build your slant. There could be whole sentences you can lift for making the guide.

Remember, you're not obligated to be profound; sometimes playful or silly words can also create strong connections. The actual word doesn't need to appear. It could be the distillation of your slant thinking. Play with it.

How to Use Your Write On Results

Let's say you did your Two Minutes on that pesky widget. In response to the third question about connecting to the greater world, you wrote, "*This widget will put the company on the map for years to come. Lots of money. People will notice.*" And your single word popped up as *fame*. You would pull those ideas out of the free-write and come up with the slant: *projected sales of this widget will rocket the company to fame and fortune.*

But what if you do this exercise and nothing productive occurs? It happens. Don't dismiss the process. Do it again. It's so short, you might try several times. If you hate everything you've babbled, lower your standards. Any guide sentence, no matter how weak, is a start. You can make it stronger later.

Sometimes the length of this exercise seems too short. Occasionally I've extended the time if my fingers don't want to quit. However, it's better to stop on time and plan to repeat the exercise after a break.

Here's why: I've discovered there are consequences if I don't stop when the timer goes off. It's like I've broken a promise to myself. When I next try the exercise, the words don't flow as easily. It's as if that inner well where the babble comes from is restricted. On the other hand, if I keep my promise, the swift act of short free-writing on a regular basis seems to enlarge the well—the more you pull from it, the more it delivers.

When to Construct a Cable-Car Sentence

The timing for when to work on a cable-car sentence will depend on your individual writing process. In the introduction to the THINK section, we talked about different writing routines and what works for planners, plungers, as well as matchers—those who combine both techniques.

Planners

If you are more comfortable knowing which direction your words will travel ahead of time, create a cable-car sentence before you launch. And if you are the kind of writer who must edit as you go, that guide sentence will be there to dictate your choices.

Plungers

You know who you are. You write in order to find out what you're thinking. Go right ahead. Then, afterwards, as part of your sifting through your inelegant, but aptly named, "vomit draft," you can build your cable-car sentence.

Matchers

You have a choice of mix and match—insert your guide sentence before you write and then create another after you write, after you've listened to yourself think. Choose which one you'll use, or meld the two together. Any way you work it, you'll have a cable-car sentence in place when you start to edit.

Where to Position the Cable-Car Sentence

As soon as you have a cable-car sentence, you can slap it like a banner at the top of your writing as a reminder. However, I think there's a better location. A student of mine suggested putting it at the end of your document, right after the last thing you've typed. So you actually start your first draft above it. That way, as you move through, when you stop to think—or get stuck—your cable-car sentence is right there in front of your eyes, reminding you of where you need to go next.

Now I always position a cable-car sentence just below what I'm typing. Want to know what's clanging away as I write this draft?

In my *THINK* chapter about *theme statements* I am saying that *you can speed up your writing process by renaming the dreaded theme statement, slicing it into three fill-in-the-blanks, and allowing your free-write to do the heavy lifting.*

The End of the Cable-Car Sentence

Okay, I've shared my cable-car sentence with you. However, your guide sentence will probably never appear in a finished piece of writing. You might share it with others as part of an editing process (see Chapter 12 for more on editing in groups), but otherwise no one needs to see it.

It's the fate of cable-car sentences to be deleted from the copy. Having done their work, they clang their way over the hill and down the other side into oblivion. Later, when you look at something you've written, you might not even remember what that sentence was. But your writing will be clearer, and your thoughts delivered in a more orderly progression, because you took that ride.

Real-World Review: Two Minutes in Action

I always save my rough notes. Below is a timed writing I did when I started work on an architecture piece for the *Oregon Quarterly*, the University of Oregon's alumni magazine. The article appeared in the Autumn 2009 edition with the title, "An Idea Floats on the Water Road—UO students help revive a derelict Kyoto canal." See if you can follow my babble.

1. **What's this writing about?** (45 seconds)
   Kyoto canal restoration collaboration btw UO prof and students—student Yoshimura showed Prof abandoned canal—his family lived by it for 700 yrs. Built 1200. When a boy, he played in ruins, found nature in puddles. Student floated idea, restore, make park, new water course runs inside old walls, a memory of old canal. About how park created. When Kyoto refurbishing infrastructure—why not build park same time. Ugly neglected.

2. **Why is it being told?** (30 seconds)
   UO lauds profs and students accomplishments. Kyoto connection—important contributions by UO landscape architecture prof and students in Kyoto design—K links to the past—Prof/students get things right, outside school—contribute beauty and honor past.

3. **How does it connect to the greater world?** (20 seconds)
   Program betw K and UO ongoing. Ky/UO linked in past designs, but nothing built. This one done—why?—connection with ancient family/history of Kyoto/city people park

needs—infrastructure must happen—a coming together—importance of landscape archi.

4. **What's the point?** (15 seconds)
   Right project/right place/right people to carry it—history not forgotten. Bring life to city.
5. **In one word, what's this about?** (10 seconds)
   LINKS

Then I wrote a cable-car sentence:

In my *spotlight article* about *the UO/Kyoto Horikawa canal restoration* I am saying *how the project linked together Professor Lovinger, Daisuki Yoshimura ('90), design students, the Kyoto government, and Kyoto's citizens to construct a new park inside an ancient canal.*

Here's how I used the results of the exercise.

1. **What's this writing about?** In the babble answer to this first question, I found the verb *floated. Floats* ended up in my title. Why try harder if the word is already delivered? It's about a canal, after all. The word *horikawa* means "water road" in Japanese, so *float* works on several levels.
2. **Why is it being told?** I thought about the alumni magazine's needs to highlight the accomplishments of both faculty and students. That raised my awareness of the WIIFM and shaped how the story unfolded.
3. **How does it connect to the greater world?** This question ties the writing to bigger, more universal implications. How does the canal project fit into the larger picture of society, trends, and life? That reminder phrase—*importance of landscape architecture*—became the summation for the article.
4. **What's the point?** This question nudged me to think how everyone came together to get this done and also helped me get to the single word of Question 5.
5. **In one word, what's this about?** I used my single word *links* for my cable-car sentence. Then in the piece, it became a metaphor. I compared the interaction of all the people who

worked on the project to the hand-forged chain links that had pulled the barges along the canal for seven centuries. And I used *links* one more time in the final paragraph:

The Horikawa Canal restoration drawings [that Professor Lovinger and the students designed] *were one link in a chain that brought the wishes of a community together, connecting pragmatic practicality with the natural world. The same principles could apply in the United States. Why not connect infrastructure refurbishing with a mandate for creating natural beauty? Both serve the public.* "*Nature isn't an object you can put a wall around,*" *says Lovinger.* "*It's about connecting people to what is beautiful and exciting.*" *And more important, he notes, it's about bringing life back to the city.* "*What was desolate and dead becomes alive.*"

Writers don't usually share their crappy notes and strange thinking. Most times we only give out what gets polished—or at least smoothed a bit. But if you understand how that clunky process takes shape, you'll be more willing to tolerate your own shaky steps. Spend a brief time doing heavy lifting and riding cable cars. It brings clarity to your thought. And that brings ease to your writing.

STRUCTURE

SECTION 2 INTRODUCTION

A ny writing will go quicker if you follow a form.

Writing to a structure is like pinning all your good ideas to an old-fashioned clothesline. Instead of a sopping ball of twisted shirts, socks, and underwear, everything is up in an orderly line, snapping in the breeze, each piece given enough room to stretch out and dry.

Structures save you time. Structures save you effort. Structures are at the heart of all creative and concise writing. And structures support everything, from blog posts to grant proposals. In this STRUCTURE section, we're going to look at how to use specific forms to your advantage—no matter what kind of writing you need to do.

Structural Supports for Every Kind of Writing

Chapter 4 examines the building block of most structures—the simple **story arc**. We'll look at why you need it and how to use it. The arc is the basis for most of the other templates in this section of the book, so it's a great place to start.

Chapter 5 takes on the **Hero's Journey**. Commonly used in fiction, this pattern can be easily applied to nonfiction writing. Once you see how this ten-step process works, you'll move ahead fast with all kinds of tasks—fact gathering, interviews, and decisions about how to tell your story.

But what if you're not writing a story? If you have to lay out information or exposition, you'll find a **variety of writing structures** in Chapter 6. With ten options and two specialized formats to choose from, you can figure out what you need and follow the form.

And finally, Chapter 7 looks at the structure of that particular writing workhorse—the **personal essay**—along with the building blocks of nonfiction scenes.

Get to know these patterns. They're shortcuts. Writing becomes easier when you give your words the support of a solid framework.

CHAPTER 4

Story Arc to the Rescue

Writing Problem: *My writing is boring and flat.*

Rx: *Climb the story arc.*

Sometimes writing suffers from the MEGO effect—it's so dull **My Eyes Glaze Over.**

But what makes it boring? Certainly some subjects—accounting, medieval Latin—seem to be inherently less exciting. But if they're aimed at the interests of those specific readers—accountants, medieval academics—the writing should garner a high WIIFM (Chapter 1). And if you've constructed a cable-car sentence to guide you (Chapter 3), everything should roll.

And yet, sometimes it doesn't. The first draft comes out flat, dull, all on one level. The information lacks form. It doesn't build.

In this chapter, we're going to take your writing to the next step by employing a simple pattern—the story arc. With the **Write On Exercise: Scar or Tattoo?** you can practice creating arcs (and write like crazy in the process). Get ideas for structuring your visual presentations with **Words to the Wise: Two Arcs and the PowerPoint**. Finally, **Real-World Review: Wrangling the Animals onto the Arc** illustrates how one writer organized her overflowing material, taking it from floundering to fantastic by adding a little bit of a curve.

What Is the Story Arc?

We all know the arc pattern, even if we haven't put a name to it. The arc is the basic building block of fiction, the structure that keeps you turning the pages of a book or glued to your seat in a theater. It goes like this: Something happens that launches the narrative. And then the story climbs and the stakes get higher. There's conflict. Drama. Even confusion. You're pulled along.

In the simplest form, here's what the pattern looks like. It starts at the bottom of the curve:

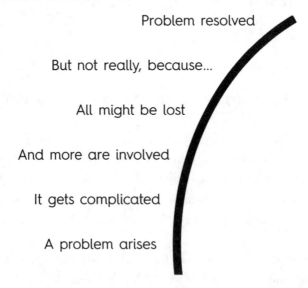

Problem resolved

But not really, because...

All might be lost

And more are involved

It gets complicated

A problem arises

I like the fact that the arc shape is dynamic. Sure, you could use a flat line to see the sequence of the information. Many people do. But the arc is a reminder that your writing is driving to a point. It's not random. One idea builds on another. Put your outline on the arc and you've got a useful shortcut that makes your job easier—and your writing more interesting.

Narrative vs. Exposition

Even though we call it a *story* arc, the structure can be applied to both narrative and exposition.

Narrative tells a story. They are a connected series of events, big or small: "And then this happened, and then that happened." Incidents build up and finally end, for better or worse, at the top of the arc. The arc visually demonstrates that the story has taken readers on a journey from where they started.

By contrast, exposition informs readers about a particular topic. In order to make things simple, I'm labeling everything that's not a story as *exposition*. There are more complicated definitions—trust me on this one—but for our purposes, think of exposition as "Just the facts, ma'am." (Thank you, *Dragnet*.) Exposition might be a collection of details about a subject. It could be a series of facts built to create an argument. It could be a description of a product. No matter the specifics, you can still use the arc for exposition.

The Arc Adds Tension

Stories possess a certain drama. Exposition doesn't. However, you can substitute simple tension for the dramatic. The arc has tension built into its shape. Don't believe me? For the best illustration of this connection, imagine you're holding a flat metal ruler. Now bend it gently. What have you done? You've put that metal under tension. And what shape have you made? An arc.

Even a small amount of tension in your writing can move it from flat to fascinating. For one thing, you've engaged the reader in the familiar arc pattern. Now they're curious. *What's going on?* You can set up readers with a series of expectations, and then pull them up the arc by presenting one issue and laying out the next. By placing your information along the arc, you'll understand the connections that link the information. And that means you'll be thinking about setting up questions in readers' minds and then addressing them. This doesn't have to be nail-biting, edge-of-your-seat tension. Subtle works. Introduce a problem and a reader wants to know: *How will this be solved?* Or, *what's the consequence of this?*

Hark, Hark, the Arc

Once you start looking for nonfiction arcs, you'll see them everywhere.

The numbered countdown, beloved by David Letterman fans, builds up tension even as the numbers go down to one. An opinion piece in the newspaper persuades readers by laying out the arguments in order of importance up the arc. Or a step-by-step how-to ("How to Replace the Toilet Flapper") rises up the arc to a finished project.

The arc is also the basis for all those TV commercials selling a $19.95 product (plus shipping and handling). An excited voiceover shouts the product's virtues, then intensifies to the "unbelievable low price!" And then jumps up again: "But wait, there's more—we'll double the offer! (Just pay separate shipping and handling.)" Sometimes two "WAITS!" follow before the ending, "Operators are standing by. Do it today!"

It's not an accident that an online video clip of elephants trying to rescue one of their babies trapped in a muddy ditch gets over twelve million views. It's a classic story arc. At first glance you're hooked on the problem. The baby—so tiny and weak—struggles to escape the ditch. It's almost under the adult's massive moving legs. *How will that baby not be stepped on? How can the others help? Will it be okay?* (Spoiler: two elephants work together to get the little guy out.)

Even without exclamation points or animal heroics, the arc will help you insert those elements of tension into your writing so your readers want to know—*what's going to happen next?* A simple arc can present an issue, build up with an exploration of solutions, and resolve at the top with a plan.

The Arc in Action

So, how do you add an arc to your writing? Let's take a look at a before and after.

Here's the beginning of a (fictional) pitch email aimed at a travel magazine. Let's imagine it's from a marketing assistant who works for a state tourist agency. The agency wants to entice people off the beaten path to the tiny town of Lily Point, Arkansas.

The assistant's initial cable-car sentence (not shared with the prospective editor) goes:

In my *piece* about *Lily Point*, I am saying that *the area has a lot of opportunities for summer recreation.*

This is what goes out in an email:

The small town of Lily Point offers much to anyone willing to leave the interstate. There are 500 miles of trails for hiking, biking, birding, and horseback riding surrounding the town. Fishing and boating opportunities are everywhere. After being outside, people can visit the small brew pubs or step into a Chinese restaurant for some authentic cuisine.

Now that's flat writing. It's a general listing. Lots of places have those amenities. Why would Lily Point stand out? If you were the travel editor, you'd probably hit delete and move on.

So let's get more specific. Let's have the assistant define the problem—*Visitors don't know about this place.* That leads to the question—*Why should they be interested in a place they don't know about?* And the answer might be—*Because undiscovered places have fewer people.* Now that's beneficial information readers might want. So the assistant offers an insider's guide to an untrammeled place readers don't know.

The unshared guide sentence might look like this:

In my *insider's guide to summer fun* I am saying that *undiscovered Lily Point offers quality outdoor experiences without the crowds.*

The beginning of the pitch email could say:

FUN THIS WAY. (The hook—catches the reader's eye.)

That sign doesn't exist on the interstate exit for Highway 58. But it should. (Reader thinks, why should it?)

Less than an hour away from that exit, the tiny town of Lily Point is the hub for quality outdoor explorations—from fiercely adventurous to serenely laid back. (Oh, that's the answer. At this point, if readers aren't interested in outdoor activities they'll stop reading. But if this is a subject they like, it sets up the next question: So what's fun about Lily Point?)

Five hundred miles of unpopulated trails meander through towering forests—350 miles are dedicated to mountain biking. (Okay, good.)

And that's just the beginning of this town's treasures. (What else?)

Water-lovers can take on whitewater challenges or backwater fishing holes. (And?)

In this quiet wilderness, you can enjoy horseback riding, take a hike, or just observe nature in solitude under a tree. (Okay. That's a good range.)

After hours, kick back in one of Lily Point's new craft brew pubs (Tasty!) *or savor a four-course authentic Chinese feast.* (Good Chinese, in Lily Point?)

No lines, no crowds, no need for reservations. (Bonus!)

Here's the insider guide to outdoor fun. (Okay, reader wants to know more.)

These short paragraphs create a dialogue between the writer and the reader. All good engagement does. The word *quality* in the beginning becomes a promise—*Really? Tell me more.* As the facts climb the arc, words like *quiet* support the idea and move up to the payoff—the bonus of solitude without mobs. Here's how those paragraphs would look on an arc. The thoughts climb like this

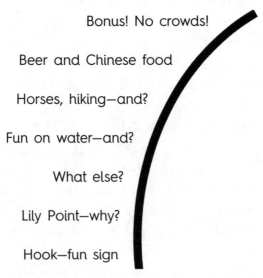

Bonus! No crowds!

Beer and Chinese food

Horses, hiking—and?

Fun on water—and?

What else?

Lily Point—why?

Hook—fun sign

I arced the first paragraphs of the pitch for brevity in this explanation, but you can pin a whole piece of writing to an arc, placing the ideas in an order that makes sense to you.

How the Arc Can Help

One of the best things about using the arc is that you immediately see when the action stops or the logic doesn't follow. An arc can give you clues for how to present your information. You can quickly discern whether your ideas are in the order you need—and then move things around if they aren't.

(Side note: The easiest way to draw an arc is on good, old-fashioned paper. I rarely form an arc on the computer—Word is so lousy at graphics.)

Arcs can be employed several ways.

Before you write a draft, you can use the arc to create a swift jot outline. Put your notes about the facts along the upward curve. If you need to, shift ideas so the material builds in a stronger sequence. Imagine an interested reader standing by your shoulder, asking questions like, *How is that going to happen?* Or, *Can you prove that?* Or simply, *Explain more.* Then bang out a first draft following the upward trajectory you've created.

Or you could pin material to the arc after you've written the first draft. Often, if you plot your writing on the arc, you'll notice what's out of place. Or where it sags. Or you see what's not conforming. If that's the case, either throw it out, or snap it into line in the rewrite.

If you're writing a piece with more complicated strands—let's say you need to create a profile about the head of a company, but also tell the company's history—you can begin by putting the facts for each topic on separate arcs. Then decide where in your writing you'll jump from one arc to another. (There's more on how to braid story strands in Chapter 7.)

I ask myself, *Does this climb? What hooks am I using to keep it moving? Does this resolve?* If the answer to any of these is no, I move things around, or I add more sentences to create questions in my reader's mind that I can then answer.

Words to the Wise: Two Arcs and the PowerPoint

The arc is particularly valuable for putting a spark into visual presentations. After you've got a guide sentence for your project, draw two arcs. The reason for two? The information you have to communicate and the best visual of that information are not the same. One is your speech and the other is your illustration. That may seem obvious, but creating notations for each arc allows you to imagine both parts before you write or put together slide pages. You'll be able to plot your course.

On the first arc, ask yourself, *What's my overall point?* Place that notation at the bottom of the first arc. Then ask yourself, *What's the best illustration that reinforces my point?* It could be a photograph, a chart, or a diagram. Place a notation about that at the bottom of the second arc. The next talking point should build on the last one. And the next visual should build as well. Keep asking yourself, *what's my next point?* And, *What's my best illustration of that point?* Sometimes it's easiest to place all your speaking notes up the arc before hopping over to the illustration notes. Or do it the other way around.

Two arcs can help if you work for a company that expects employees to put their outline notes on the slides, so that they can be shared around afterwards. If you find yourself in that culture, simply reverse the questions for the two arcs. The words that appear on your slides are the answer to the question, *What's my point?* The speech you make answers the other question, *What's the best illustration of this point?* You can come up with anecdotes or examples that clarify what's outlined on the screen.

With two arcs, you won't find yourself trapped, repeating the words on the screen that everyone can already see. Answering the questions will also narrow your focus and prevent you from weighing your presentation down with extra facts.

Write On Exercise: Scar or Tattoo?

Time: Fifteen minutes

This exercise gives you a chance to practice placing information on a story arc. I am indebted to Professor Tom Wheeler at the University of Oregon's School of Journalism and Communication who shared this scar/tattoo story prompt many years ago.

You'll need 3" x 5" cards. You can do this with sticky notes, or even scraps of paper, but the cards are heavier so they (mostly) stay where I put them. It's also possible to do this on a computer, but I think it's easier to use physical notes.

Step 1. Scar or tattoo? Think of a time in your life when you received a scar or a tattoo—your choice.

Step 2. Write one fact per card. Put one salient fact about the experience on each card. *My mother warned me not to ride that bike.* Answer questions like, When did it happen? *Early morning.* Where were you? *My aunt's house.* Who was there? How old were you? What started the incident? How did you/others react? Why did it happen? Keep the answers brief.

Step 3. Arc your facts. Now arrange your cards on an imaginary arc (or draw one on a large piece of paper). In what order do you want to tell this story? It doesn't have to be chronological, although you could start at the beginning. *I slipped the bike out of the garage.* Or you could start with the most dramatic moment: *The driver's face was the last thing I saw.* Then arrange the rest of the cards to build back up to that place. Try it several ways.

Step 4. Free-write. (5 minutes) Choose your favorite beginning and start your story as a timed writing.

Step 5. Start differently. (5 minutes) Now move another card to the bottom of the arc. Rearrange the cards accordingly. Write another five-minute free-write with that beginning.

Step 6. Review your writing. If working with a partner, share your observations. Did your two stories climb the arc in the way you planned? Was there a place where one went flat? Did you stick to the facts you already had or go off on a diversion? What happened with a different beginning?

The subject of getting a scar or tattoo has built-in drama. It's personal. For most people, their stories come rolling out easily. In other areas of less intense writing, much of what you need to communicate can roll out the same way if you use an arc.

How the Arc Can Change Your Focus

That last question in the "Scar or Tattoo" exercise—*What happened with a different beginning?*—is one of the most important. Your opening affects not only how the story gets told, but also the slant of the writing. It affects what you promise the reader.

For instance, if you were writing about getting a tattoo, you might start at the bottom of the arc with the fact, *I was barely seventeen.* Then you'd be promising that this would be a story about youthful decisions. But if you started off with, *My friends met me at the bar*, the slant might shift to drunken indiscretions. Or if you began, *I walked past that tat shop every day and never went in before*, you would be telling a tale of new worlds explored.

The Arc Comes in Many Sizes

Arcs can delineate all kinds of information, from a single paragraph to an enormous report. Well-written paragraphs build on an arc with each sentence launching from the last. In turn, those paragraphs could each be positioned along the larger arc of the whole piece. Sections of writing can also be pinned to an arc. For example, chapters arc up into books.

I think about writing arcs like fractals in nature. Fractals are the mathematical expression of similar shapes that get repeated in ever smaller or larger patterns. For instance, a tree's twigs grow out of the branches at roughly the same angle as the branches grow out of the trunk. In the same way, the pattern of a nautilus seashell is the same as the starry arms in our spiral nebula galaxy. We've evolved in a world of astonishing patterns. And it turns out, we prefer patterns instead of chaos.

By adding the arc pattern to the chaos of your own thoughts, you have an instant connection with your reader. The arc is familiar. Whether your reader notices your structure or not—and we hope they don't—there's a level of comfort within it. And by using it, you reach a level of comfort with what you write.

Real-World Review: Wrangling the Animals Onto the Arc—One Writer's Dilemma Solved

The animals started it all. Twenty years ago, Deanna Mather Larson moved to the sprawling acreage she and her husband dubbed Menagerie Ranch. Animals of all kinds—abandoned dogs and cats, abused horses, scruffy llamas, and wandering goats—ended up on the ranch.

The animals and their struggles became totally engrossing. Deanna started sharing their stories in twice-monthly radio spots, "Tales of Menagerie Ranch," for her local NPR station. Because she was also freelance writing for magazines as varied as *Old House Journal* and *Applied Clinical Trials*, she decided the next step would be to write a book about the ranch.

She put together a rough first draft, but when she started editing, she got stuck. "I didn't know how to cut it," she explains. "It had all the little details and minutia of ranch life. I wanted to make it simpler." She put the draft away.

But the animals and their stories kept coming. Mighty Lester, the amorous goat, tore down fences, stalls, and even a barn door when separated from his harem. A pig, Flower Ann, ensconced herself in the laundry room. And then there was Barney, the cat-killing basset hound the couple rescued from death row. A white cat named Bert taught Barney that cats were permanently off-limits. People kept asking Deanna how she learned to manage all these animals.

"At that point, I realized I had another story to tell—mine," Deanna says. "I started out a city-born girl. My animals gave me instant feedback. I learned my skills at the paws, hooves, and sometimes teeth, of my critters."

Then a third storyline emerged. "I knew if you had a business, you could deduct all the expenses from your taxes," Deanna says. So she figured she and her husband could be ranchers and grow hay. They had a fifteen-year deadline to turn a profit. It was a gamble. If they didn't succeed by then, they'd owe massive amounts in back taxes, with the looming possibility of being forced to sell the ranch to meet their obligations.

Deanna reconsidered the book. How could she keep all those strands of ranch life from jumbling together? That's when she called upon the story arc. Or in this case, three of them. She plotted her whole book on three separate arcs.

The first arc involved the animals. Each one had a chapter where their individual stories climbed up the arc to a satisfying resolve. "I'd kept a chart of when they arrived and when they departed," Deanna says. "That developed the pattern."

The second arc was her education. She started out a greenhorn and ended up pack leader for her motley tribe. Her accumulation of knowledge built up step by step on its own arc.

The third arc involved the struggles to make the ranch pay. Raising hay, growing daffodils, and selling cashmere wool all failed. The tension grew through the years with worries about the IRS deadline until Deanna finally discovered a steady source of income for the ranch.

The whole book builds in an overall chronological arc, covering the fifteen years it took for Menagerie Ranch to beat the IRS deadline. In every chapter, elements of all three story arcs are included. The animals are the main thread. The other two stories are woven in.

At first it was difficult to write, she says. "I thought—where do I start? Where's the apex? I rewrote a lot."

But the more Deanna relied on the arcs, the more obvious it became where the information belonged. "Having the three arcs made it easier," she says. "Funny how it all came together."

CHAPTER 5

The Hero's Journey

Writing Problem: *I've got a real-life story. How do I tell it?*

Rx: *Borrow a structure from the fictional Hero's Journey.*

When you need to tell a story, it's easy to get overwhelmed by your material. Maybe you've been assigned to describe how your neighborhood group got started, or how your company solved a major problem, or how a grant made all the difference for a specific community. You've done your research and interviews. You've got your facts and figures. Your next goal should be to write a first draft as quickly and efficiently as possible. You sit down to compose.

And that's when you can get hijacked by the material you've gathered.

What's the best way to start? Which ideas are irrelevant? What's really the point of all those interviews? How do you lay out this narrative? Suddenly, all that information becomes paralyzing.

The good news: you can tame your material with the classic Hero's Journey paradigm. While this storytelling pattern is most often used in fiction, it's also a great way to structure a nonfiction story.

The Hero's Journey solves problems like:

- Not knowing if you have gathered enough information—or too much.
- Not having a strong focus.
- Not staying on track.
- Not being able to decide in what order the story should be told.
- Not maintaining a strong sense of drive.
- Not seeing where the story starts or ends.

The **Illustration: Ten-Step Hero's Journey** gives a visual reference. After you're familiar with the structure, we'll look at real-world writing examples of how to use each step in the Hero's Journey. The structure also comes in handy if you have to conduct an interview—the **Cheat Sheet: The Best Questions** gives you ready-made interview questions for any occasion. The **Write On Exercise: Plot the Journey** helps you get hands-on with this concept, and a **Real-World Review: The Hero's Journey and the Garden** demonstrates the steps in action.

Take the Hero's Journey

In the classic fiction form, we follow a character as they move out of ordinary life to face a challenge on a previously unknown path. Lessons are learned, allies and enemies are met, and obstacles are overcome—or sometimes not. By the end, the hero returns, often a changed person, with new knowledge to impart to others.

In his definitive 1949 book on the subject, *The Hero with a Thousand Faces*, Joseph Campbell points out that the Hero's Journey is found in the myths of practically all cultures around the world, living and dead. It's not much of a jump to say human beings are hard-wired to recognize this construct. Perhaps it's embedded in our DNA. So why not use this familiar form in nonfiction writing?

I'm using the term *hero* as gender universal—it refers to both men and women. In fact, the hero doesn't even have to be an actual human being. Almost any object—an organization, a building, a work project, a piece of art, a natural phenomenon, a political movement—can be the hero.

This flexibility means you can use the Hero's Journey in all kinds of stories, including a company update, a letter explaining why donors should open their wallets, or a blog post about a specific event in your life.

If you have a story to tell, no matter how short or long, the Hero's Journey can help.

The Ten-Step Hero's Journey

The number of steps in the Hero's Journey varies, but for simplicity, I have chosen ten. Typically, the fiction form is illustrated as a circle, or a clock face, with the hero going clockwise around the pattern. Step 7 (the dark hour) appears at the bottom in the six o'clock position. I prefer to use an open arc because I think it is easier to visualize the story as it climbs upward.

10. Hero becomes a teacher.

9. Hero meets the ultimate challenge.

8. Hero takes a leap of faith.

7. Hero experiences the dark hour
of the soul/the dark wood.

6. Hero meets the problem head on
and is defeated.

5. Hero learns new skills
and knowledge.

4. Hero gathers allies, mentors, and
enemies along the road.

3. Hero accepts the challenge.

2. Hero turns down the challenge.

1. Hero confronted by a challenge.

Hero's Journey Structure in Fiction

Any moviegoer will recognize the Hero's Journey. Thousands of well-known films use it, including *Star Wars*—George Lucas actually consulted with Joseph Campbell before he launched the first film of his epic.

I've chosen the film *Legally Blonde* to illustrate the ten steps. Whether you love or hate it, *Legally Blonde* perfectly fits the paradigm because screenwriters Karen McCullah Lutz and Kirsten Smith conscientiously followed the form. Once you see the ten steps in action, you can apply them when you're writing or editing your nonfiction drafts.

Step 1—The hero is confronted by a challenge.

Step 1 is the inciting incident. It's the point where ordinary expectations are interrupted. *Legally Blonde* kicks off with popular sorority sister Elle Woods arriving at a fancy restaurant where she thinks her boyfriend Warner will propose—the ring on her finger will be culmination of Elle's successful undergraduate career. Instead, Warner breaks up with her before trotting off to Harvard Law School.

Step 2—The hero turns down the challenge.

In Western culture's fiction, this refusal to accept the challenge is usually based on a character flaw that will come back to bite the protagonist when things get really bad (Step 7). In *Legally Blonde*, Elle deeply believes that she can only achieve status and contribute to society if she marries Mr. Right. This is her character weakness. She reacts to her failure to snag Warner by retreating to her bed for a week with a box of chocolates.

Step 3—The hero accepts the challenge.

Reasons always exist for the hero to take up the journey. Sometimes the hero is forced into it through circumstance. Sometimes the hero makes a choice. In the movie, Elle is of the generation who've been told they can do anything. She decides to get Warner back by attending Harvard Law School too. Against improbable odds (and with the help of a perky application video) she pulls it off. This is where Elle crosses the threshold into a different world.

Step 4—The hero gathers allies, mentors, and enemies along the road.

This step is familiar in many fiction forms, from fairy tales to murder mysteries. In her new world at Harvard, Elle meets her first friend, Paulette, a goofy manicurist. She also acquires an eventual love interest and a collection of odd-lot fellow law students. More important, Elle encounters a hard-nosed professor who kicks her out of class the first day for not being prepared. This woman is a mentor who demands more from our hero.

Step 5—The hero learns new skills and knowledge.

In fiction, Steps 4 and 5 are often repeated several times, raising the stakes with both wins and losses. These two steps push the plot up the arc of complication. Lessons may be easy or difficult. Elle Woods learns how to study, how to dress, and how to answer the demanding prof's questions. She experiences conflicts, losses, and small victories, such as helping her friend Paulette rescue her dog from an abusive ex-boyfriend.

Step 6—The hero meets the problem head on and is defeated.

All the action is leading up the arc to this point. With Elle, that moment comes during her first trial experience. Callahan, her sleazy trial lawyer professor, hits on her. She smacks him down, but thinks she has only made it this far because of her looks. Her precarious new identity is shattered.

Step 7—The hero experiences the dark hour of the soul.

Also referred to as "the dark wood," Step 7 explores those times of greatest agony or pain. In fiction, this point often coincides with the all-is-lost moment because character drives the plot. It sets up the question, How will they get out of this one? With *Legally Blonde*, Elle concludes she is unworthy to be a person in her own right. (This connects back to her weakness in Step 2.) She quits school and seeks solace one last time with Paulette at the manicurist's salon.

Step 8—The hero takes a leap of faith.

The answer to the dark wood question—how will they get out of this one?—can take three different forms. The first way, the character looks within—this is an up-by-the-bootstraps push from the deepest reserves. In the second possibility, the hero gets help from others—remember all those met along the road? Or with the third choice, the hero receives assistance from of a higher power or inspiration. In *Legally Blonde*, the professor who kicked Elle out of class just happens to be having her hair done at the same salon. She confronts Elle: "If you're going to let one stupid prick ruin your life, you're not the student I thought you were." It's a statement of sisterhood (help from others) and also the use of a higher power. After all, to a law student, the professor *is* a higher power.

Step 9—The hero meets the ultimate challenge.

This is the moment of triumph or defeat. In comedies, heroes prevail; in tragedies, heroes lose. The structure remains the same. With *Legally Blonde*, Elle rallies. She confounds the sleazy law professor, goes back into the courtroom, and wins the case by calling on her authentic self—which includes her knowledge of designer shoes and hair perm chemicals. She is cheered by her friends on the courthouse steps.

Step 10—The hero becomes a teacher.

In many stories around the world the hero crosses back over the threshold and returns home to share the knowledge and experience with others. If this step doesn't sound familiar, it's because it isn't. Culturally, Americans tend to prefer the triumph over the lessons learned. Often our stories cut off this part of the Hero's Journey and the narrative ends with the victory of Step 9. However, *Legally Blonde* includes Step 10. In a coda graduation scene, Elle gives the shortest speech in law school history. She is stepping back over the threshold to meet the real world beyond school. Her what-I-learned-in-the-last-three-years homily completes the pattern.

Hero's Journey in Real Life

You can fit your nonfiction narrative into the steps of the Hero's Journey. Here are examples of how to adapt the pattern. Please note that any one, or several, of these steps could be the focus of your writing.

Step 1—Meets the challenge.

For writers, the ordinary part of your material is the "before," as in, "before the storm," "before the Internet," or "before this company's inception." Then you need to examine what happened to change that. The inciting incident may be a whole story in itself.

Step 2—Rejects the challenge.

All heroes have a weakness. Look out for it. People may have flaws, groups might harbor doubts, movements may contain contradictions. With organizations—or even countries—the fault line usually occurs at the time of the founding. For instance, the United States was founded with a split in philosophy. Much has been written about this founding fracture. By tracing back to it, people explain problems the country faces now. Be alert to these points of conflict. Drama makes your story a compelling read.

Step 3—Accepts challenge.

When you gather your information, note when and how the challenge is taken up. Sometimes the person you're writing about embraces the future with no worries or doubt. Other times, many difficulties emerge before a decision is made. Either way, a little more digging on your part may uncover interesting reasons why the pathway was chosen. Even the easy choice can be relevant. Sometimes what isn't there (no stumbling blocks) can be more revealing than what is. You get to point it out. Alternatively, easy beginnings might foreshadow real trouble down the line in Step 7.

Step 4—Gathers allies, enemies.

This is significant when you're working on nonfiction profiles and histories. With a company profile, you could zoom in for a close-up on the organization (the hero) and the person you're profiling becomes the ally who helps the business shine. Or, if you were writing with a wider shot and incorporating more of the ten steps in a history, it would be important to note who and what helped or thwarted the effort. This step helps you find the auxiliary players you may need to interview.

Step 5—Learns new skills.

When you're writing, this is the "stuff happens" part. Mistakes are made. Knowledge is gained. In profiles, if you focus on this step, you may find out how people would have done things differently if they could repeat the process. People or organizations might start with one mission, and for a series of reasons, end up with another. Here's the place where that happens.

Step 6—Meets challenge, fails.

In real-life stories, this is the greatest challenge—for a person, a business, an idea, or an institution. Everything hinges on this. The test can come from the outside—market shifts bring new and unexpected competition for an entrepreneur. Or it can emerge from inside and be based on the flaw you identified in Step 2. For instance, a company might have an ideological split: will they go in the direction of a proprietary product or open source?

Step 7—Experiences dark hour.

In nonfiction, these are the times when a person, a business, an idea, or an institution can seriously falter. The future looks bleak. Nothing goes right. As a writer, look for these points. In interviews, be prepared with questions about these experiences, and then listen carefully. People may tell you about their dark hours in veiled terms. Some find it hard to admit anything ever happened. Not all histories have this moment, but most do.

By knowing the Hero's Journey structure, you can listen, wait, and not jump in with the next question right away. You may be rewarded with a gripping tale.

Step 8—Takes a leap of faith.

It's important to examine this turning point. If you know about the dark hour, then you may discover through your research and interviews the answers to how they got out of the chaos. Did they rely on internal strength, help from others, or a higher power? It might be all three. Readers are always interested in how a recovery happens.

Step 9—Meets challenge, wins (loses).

This glory moment in any nonfiction piece is key. In a story that incorporates many of the ten steps, everything is rolling up to this point. What constitutes the win? What physical details can show readers the triumph? It could be a series of amazing statistics or descriptions of how people act. You might use excited dialogue you have witnessed to convey the moment. Or instead of covering a win, you might need to report on losses, especially as a cautionary tale. Then you are looking at the consequences of actions that have failed.

Step 10—Returns as a teacher.

In nonfiction work, this is an important step—especially when you're writing about people looking back on their own legacy. Step 10 is the point where people reflect on how they, or their company, or their ideas have arrived at achievement. This is the place to explore take-away concepts readers could apply to other situations. You can raise the WIIFM here (Chapter 1). You show the specifics of one story, and draw wider connections and conclusions.

The Hero's Journey in Action

Let's say you need to write a story explaining how your company created a successful menu-planning app for schools. Here's how the Hero's Journey might shape your piece. All but Step 10 is included.

The Making of an App

In 2010, the US Congress passed the Healthy, Hunger-Free Kids (HHFK) Act for public schools. That same year, food service consultant Frances Goldstein found herself facing a decision. Frances had spent 30 years helping schools plan menus, the last 10 as president of her own company. Now the HHFK Act was going to require districts across the country to meet a brand new set of nutritional standards (Step 1—Confronts challenge).

Frances had two options. She could retire and let the new regulations be someone else's problem (Step 2—Rejects challenge). *Or she could develop a software tool to help her clients meet the changes. She'd have "one last really fun project to work on." Frances chose the fun project, and the Complete Menu Planning (CMP) app was born* (Step 3—Accepts challenge).

When development began, Frances wanted to create an app that would make menu planning easy. Hard to do. As it stood, the process was complex, difficult to calculate, and required outrageous amounts of time-consuming reporting.

For the app, Frances and her team settled on Drupal, an open-source development framework. They paid the first developers (Step 4—Gathers allies) *to roll out an initial version, which launched in June 2012* (Step 5—Acquires new skills).

Customers were pleased. However, when the scale of the operation expanded in 2013, the entire system ground to a halt. The original developers said they'd done all they could. The system simply couldn't handle any more traffic (Step 6—Meets challenge, fails).

This was the point where Frances seriously considered going back to her retirement option (Step 7—Dark hour). *However, she felt she couldn't let down all those school districts. So she and her team rallied and began the search for new developers* (Step 8—Leap of faith).

They came to High Flyers. Our shop specializes in large-scale Drupal development. We worked to overhaul the app, bringing it forward from Drupal 6 to Drupal 7. We restructured the software so that it would be well equipped to handle rapid growth (Step 9— Meets ultimate challenge, wins).

Now, version 2 of the CMP app goes live at 165 districts across the country. Frances and her team continue to work with High Flyers to add more features and functionality. CMP allows food service staff to get back to the most important part of their jobs: planning and serving healthy, delicious meals.

Not all parts of the Hero's Journey need to be used. You make the call about which you want. For another example, here's the beginning of a fictive donor ask letter. With few words, it echoes the familiar path.

Lucinda, a single mom, was struggling to provide for her two small kids. When she lost her job (Step 1—Confronts challenge), *it felt like the ground gave way beneath her. The bills piled up* (Step 2— Rejects challenge to continue). *She had no one to turn to. Nowhere to go.*

Then she found our organization (Step 3—Accepts challenge). *We welcomed her in with a hug and a cup of coffee* (Step 4— Gathers allies). *This overwhelmed mom told us her story. With your support, we were able to give her groceries, clothes for the kids, and counseling for how to handle her bills* (Step 5—Learns new skills).

Now Lucinda has control of her finances. In fact, she's now helping other women learn the same skills through a community support group she created (Step 10—Returns as a teacher). *Because you gave, something extraordinary happened.*

Write On Exercise: Plot the Journey

Time: Twenty minutes

In this exercise, you'll organize your material on the Hero's Journey arc.

Step 1. Gather your material. This can come from a rough draft (plungers), from research notes you have collected (planners), or from a combination (matchers).

Step 2. Number your notes. Go through and assign numbers from the ten steps to the bits and pieces. Don't over think this. Just order them on first impulse. Make decisions based on chronology. What happened in the beginning? What came next? You can always move a chunk to a different numbered step later. Skip any parts that you can't make an easy decision about.

Step 3. Draw an arc. Start near the bottom left side of the paper and draw the arc up toward the top right side. Do this on the computer or freehand. Neatness does not count. An 8½" x 11" sheet of paper works well. If you have lots of material, a larger piece of drawing paper holds more. Number the steps up the arc on the inside of the curve so you have more room to write on the outside.

Step 4. Place the information on the arc. Go through your notes and assign material to one of the corresponding ten steps. Write short word reminders from your numbered notes. Some people use sticky notes. If a certain step gets crowded, create a separate arc for that step, and write in everything that pertains to it. For example, finding everything that fits in Step 5 (learns new skills) allows you to closely compare the facts and to judge which are the most important to the whole story. After everything is on, go back to those bits where you were undecided. It may be clearer now where they should go. Or, leave them out and pick them up later if you need them.

Step 5. Decide on a focus. You may notice some steps have very little. This can help you in two ways. You may have to garner more information. Or you may choose to focus on the story you already have. This can lead you to your cable-car sentence (Chapter 3) if you haven't created one yet.

Step 6. Choose an order for your story. Your writing does not have to be laid out chronologically. Now that you can see it, you can determine where to start. Which step on the arc will launch your writing most vividly? Make a jot outline or another arc based on the order you want. Try launching several different ways. This shortcut saves you time and grief with both first drafts and subsequent edits.

Step 7. Share the process and move on. If you have a writing buddy (Chapter 12), take turns talking about the decisions that went into the construction of your arc. Offer other possible ways to formulate your partner's work. If you're writing alone, allow a day to pass—if you can—then look at your decisions with new eyes. Now write. You can be confident that the choices you've made will result in a more coherent draft.

Problems Solved with the Hero's Journey

Let's go back to the disorganization problems that started this chapter and examine how the Hero's Journey paradigm can sort them out.

Not Knowing if You Have Enough—or Too Much

By plotting your material on the Hero's Journey arc, you can easily see where you have holes. These gaps can signal that you need to gather more—even though you thought you had it all. You can also see which steps are crowded with information. This is especially useful if you're someone who loves to research but hates to write. When you find yourself turning up the same facts, it's time to stop and get on with it.

Not Having a Strong Focus

You don't need all ten steps to be effective—sometimes the best stories only drill down into one or two steps. By seeing where the facts lie on the structure, you can decide where you want to focus. That decision will narrow your ideas to the most important aspects. You can pluck out the extraneous before you write your first draft—that's a major time-saver.

Not Staying on Track

You can use the paradigm to keep from repeating yourself or wandering. If you plug your facts and observations into the arc, you'll immediately spot the repetitions. Then you can make choices. The same is true for wandering away from your message. On the arc, you see where you've gone off track. It's simpler to remove information now, before you have intertwined it into your writing. If you find you've left out something important, you can always jump back and locate it on the arc.

Not Maintaining a Strong Sense of Drive

Drive comes from drama. The Hero's Journey is inherently dramatic. When you plotted facts and information on a single arc in Chapter 4, you automatically invested more tension into a flat or boring story. And each of the ten steps in the Hero's Journey consists of its own arc, naturally loaded with conflict. For those writers who tend to avoid discord, the points of crisis may give you just the grabber you need.

Not Being Able to Decide in What Order the Story Should Be Told

Visualizing the structure allows you to experiment with the ordering of information. Try moving chunks around freely. What if you started with Step 7 (all is lost)? Then you could loop back to Step 1 (meets challenge) to find out how they got in trouble. Or perhaps Step 4 (finds allies) has an emotional charge you like. You could start there and then jump back to Step 1 and forward to Step 8 (leap of faith) to show how those allies helped meet the challenge.

Not Seeing Where the Story Starts or Ends

Beginnings and endings become more obvious after you've played around with the arc. You will have more of a focus for your start because of your experiments in various step progressions. Endings are created by eliminating everything that doesn't serve your story. It may not be exactly where you'll start and stop your final edit, but if you work with this structure, your choices will be solid as you write your draft.

What If My Writing Doesn't Fit the Pattern?

It happens. Sometimes you gather facts that seem to fall outside of the structure. By knowing the Hero's Journey, you can note the outliers—the information you have that doesn't fit. That disparity may give you the perfect launch for your writing. Often, because readers innately know the structure, you can play against their expectations.

Perhaps you're working on a profile, but the person will never tell you the name of a friend or colleague who helped along the way (Step 4). That person sees himself as a complete lone wolf. With that subject, you can create interest by highlighting the opposite of what readers assume. Reverse the idea of help along the way (Step 4) and point out that lonely aspect.

For another piece, you might meet a relentless optimist, somebody who would never admit to having a moment of doubt, let alone despair, for herself or her organization (Step 7). Knowing this doesn't fit, you might question others around her—is her upbeat attitude real or not? And then you can focus on that. If she has a hidden downside, that's one kind of story. If she's as sunny as everyone says, you can again challenge readers' assumptions about a disaster (Step 7) and illustrate that. Are there consequences to eternal optimism?

Or, perhaps you're writing about your own experience, and everything seems far too nuanced to fit into any pattern. In writing about your life, you may have trouble placing the many details on the arc. If so, pick the three most important facts that resonate with you. Decide where they belong in the ten steps. Then you'll know which part of your journey you want to examine, and which other parts you could sum up with a sentence, just to get you from here to there. Sometimes you might notice thoughts, feelings, or incidents you don't want to put on the arc. Fine. Don't do it. But be aware of the holes where you have left out information. Those spaces will shape the story you do want to tell.

If everything you have seems completely random, consider that it might not be a story. It's only now, after you've wrestled with it, that you may understand that. If so, go on to Chapter 6 for choices about how to lay out the facts readers need.

When things don't fit, or are absent, it's a great message: examine your material. By working with the timeless pattern, and looking at what goes up the arc and what doesn't, you save yourself time and effort when it comes to getting out a first draft.

The Hero's Journey Guides the Interview

Interviewing a real live person can be seriously intimidating. You don't want to be seen as nosy, overly curious, or stepping on someone's unexplored boundaries. So let the Hero's Journey be your guide.

Instead of inventing your interview from scratch, use the 10 steps as the basis for your questions. (The sidebar Cheat Sheet: Interview the Hero shows you how.) This saves valuable writing time, and it can help with a host of other interview issues.

Above all, this structure lets you get out of your own way. It allows you to take a less personal tone, even when dealing with emotional material. It also keeps you from letting your own biases color the questions. Many an interviewer has missed the story because they were charging down preconceived avenues of inquiry.

The paradigm also lets you pick up details you might have overlooked. Once the 10 steps are familiar, you'll start to recognize people's seemingly random responses. You'll know exactly where they fit on the arc—and in your writing. For instance, if you are aware of Step 4—Gains allies and enemies, you will never overlook researching or asking about secondary interviews of others around the issue.

When you rely on the Hero's Journey, you can also be more at ease asking improvised follow-ups—those unplanned questions that arise because something interesting has been said and you want to know more. For instance, let's say you are interviewing someone about the founding of a school. It turns out this board member is also a leader of a motorcycle club. You'll want to jump on that fact with follow-ups. You might ask—when did you start riding? (Step 1—Confronts challenge) Or, do you think there any similar values shared between motorcycle culture and schools? (Step 10—Returns as teacher)

People often think deeply about their passions, but they don't talk about their thoughts until someone shows an interest. What you elicit could become the whole point of your piece.

And because the Hero's Journey is embedded in all of us, we tend to tell stories about ourselves and the things around us using this familiar paradigm, whether we recognize it or not. So you can have confidence that your interview questions will usually be greeted by people who already think in the same pattern.

The Overlapping Hero's Journeys in Our Lives

After all this talk of writing to the pattern, it's important to remember that our lives are complex, quirky, and anything but linear. A single story may fit the model, but everyone's experiences are multifaceted and multi-dimensional. Human beings and their endeavors take many complicated journeys at the same time. Anyone or anything could be traveling on parallel journeys and be at different stages in each of them.

Cheat Sheet: Interview the Hero

I've set the following questions up as a profile interview, but you can easily turn them into queries about inanimate objects, communities, ideas—anything with a story attached to it. When creating your own questions, allow your curiosity to rule. If you want to know more, most times readers will too.

Step 1—Confronts a challenge.

- What made you start to do XYZ?
- How did you come to see that this was important?
- What attracted you to this project?

Step 2—Turns it down.

- Were you on another path at first?
- Was this the first thing you wanted to do?

Step 3—Accepts the challenge.

- What circumstances helped you decide to do what you did?
- How did you change your mind?
- What made you finally say yes?

Step 4—Gathers allies, mentors, and enemies.

- Who assisted you along the way?
- Who/what blocked you?
- Who did you learn from?
- What were your influences?

Step 5—Learns new skills.

- What expertise did you have to learn?
- What mistakes/wrong assumptions did you make?
- How did you correct that?

Step 6—Meets the problem head on and loses.

- Tell me about the time of your greatest challenge/ struggle.
- How did that happen?
- What led up to that?

Step 7—Dark hour of the soul.

- Was there a time when you thought, "This isn't going to happen?"
- Did you ever have serious doubts about what you were doing?
- Did others? (There may or may not be a connection with Step 2.)

Step 8—Leap of faith.

- How did you get around that obstacle?
- What happened that helped you solve the problem?
- How did you figure out what to do?

Step 9—Hero wins.

- When did you know this is going to work?
- What was your moment of greatest fulfillment/ triumph?
- What changed as a result?

Step 10—Hero becomes teacher.

- What have you learned from this challenge?
- What would you tell others?
- What do you know now you didn't know then?

Consider someone just entering the workforce. This person is traversing the threshold into a new world. Behind him lies Steps 1 through 3—the process of getting through school or training. Ahead of him are Steps 4 and 5—gathering allies and skills. At the same time, the new worker is completing another journey. Childhood and adolescence are over. He has arrived at Step 10—what he learned growing up. He will probably tell parts of Step 10 for the rest of his life, even as he goes forward on many other journeys.

As a writer, you can use this complexity to your advantage. Look for the telling details that indicate which journey you are following. Understand the different paths people are on concurrently. For example, someone could be attaining the height of her career on one track and also just be starting out—say, learning to kayak—on another track. When you're writing, those facts could be placed next to each other to illustrate certain characteristics. You might point out that she attacks her kayaking lessons with the same doggedness that marked the early days of opening her business.

Writing a first draft can feel a bit like marching into your own dark wood. But if you have a story to tell, take a few minutes to work with this timeless structure. It can become your ally—one that clears your way for better writing and easier editing.

Real-World Review: The Hero's Journey and the Garden

Here's how the structure saved the day

At the beginning of my magazine writing career, I got a call from an editor at *Sunset, the Magazine of Western Living*. I was assigned to do an article about a garden that had won the Oprah Winfrey "Nightmare Backyard Makeover Contest." I drove to the suburbs outside Portland, Oregon, for a look.

The garden was nicely designed. Trees, shrubs, flowers, and grass wrapped around the back of a ranch-style home. However, the contest, the makeover, and the TV segment had occurred almost two years before—seriously old news. "As seen on TV," even with the Oprah effect, wasn't much of a hook for *Sunset* readers. I tried not to let the homeowner see my disappointment.

I had no story.

I couldn't go back to the editor—he was renowned for crankiness—and tell him all we had was a leafy suburban yard. I'd never get another assignment.

I stood there in the middle of the neatly mowed lawn, with one small fact about TV makeovers niggling at me. I knew that, unlike indoor home remodels, most TV gardens do not last. Usually constructed in a hurried three-day time frame, the makeovers either die from a lack of long-term planning—no sprinklers or good topsoil—or they outgrow their spaces and turn into jungles.

This one had lived. This one had lived happily ever after.

Now I had a fairy tale hook. And fairy tales are Hero's Journeys. Just like that, everything fell into place.

The sad garden with its single dead Douglas fir tree was the hero. Winning the nightmare contest was the challenge (Steps 1–3). The designer and the builder who did the careful work that allowed the garden to thrive were the allies (Step 4). The new plant material—a bit of a stretch—was knowledge gained (Step 5).

Because this was a transformative story, I chose Cinderella as the controlling metaphor. Oprah became the fairy godmother. The dark woods and the return (Steps 7–8) were not there, but I got a great quote from the designer that summed up meeting the ultimate challenge (Step 9): "I'd done a garden makeover in three days, but Oprah's people said, 'You have to do it in two.'"

The results of the garden's transformation (Step 10) were celebrated in the description of the design and the plants. Of course, lush photography supported the theme.

It turned into the easiest piece I'd ever written.

Titled "Cinderella Makeover," the article went on to appear in several regional editions of *Sunset*, as well as a couple of books. The happy editor told me it attained one of the highest reader-interest scores in the magazine's history. I went on to a long and productive writing relationship with *Sunset*.

Deconstruction alert: You've probably noticed that what I've just told you is also in the form of a Hero's Journey. It's an innate pattern—even if the subject is a garden makeover. The template works. And if you've gotten any insight from reading this, we've arrived together at Step 10.

CHAPTER 6

Other Structures, Other Forms

Writing Problem: *I'm not telling a story. What structure should I use?*

Rx: *Twelve structures get the job done.*

The previous chapters of the STRUCTURE section covered the basic structural building block—the story arc—and looked at the Hero's Journey to tell nonfiction narratives. But often, storytelling is not your main goal. You're called upon to make a request, outline a problem, or persuade others to take your point of view. You're dealing in facts, figures, supporting details, arguments, and opinions.

This kind of writing needs other structures—and that's what this chapter is all about. We'll go through ten main options and two bonus templates for specific jobs: the pitch and the review.

Cheat Sheet: Uses for Structures offers suggestions for deciding which of the options would be best for your writing. **Wind Up the Pitch** gives you a pattern any time you have to offer your writing ideas to editors.

The **Write On Exercise: Plot Three Ways** encourages you look beyond your first impulse, and the **Real-World Review: A Mile Wide and an Inch Deep** tells about how my most hated writing structure could be your most useful.

Structures to Mix and Match

These 10 structures (in alphabetical order) allow you to organize your facts into a coherent presentation. Often, depending on your subject, one type will fit your needs better than the others.

1. Cause/Effect
2. Chronological
3. Classification/Division
4. Compare/Contrast
5. Descriptive
6. Inverted Pyramid
7. List/Number
8. Problem/Solution
9. Question/Answer
10. Sequential

To make them easy to understand, I've divided these patterns into ten distinct categories. However, you can mix multiple categories within the same piece of writing. The more familiar you become with this way of working, the more choices you'll be able to make. Don't worry—there's no right or wrong way to use these forms. If your material doesn't fit into one, try another. Consider each as a suggestion. It's up to you to decide which way you'll play it.

1. Cause/Effect

Any time you can directly connect specific facts to specific results, you can use the cause/effect structure. (A type of this structure also goes by the name of deductive/inductive reasoning and is often used in academic and scientific writing.)

There are two ways to shape cause and effect. First, you could start with the cause. You lay out a description of the given facts or situation (cause) and follow up with the resulting impacts (effect) as you climb the arc to a conclusion. This is good for examining the question *how did this happen?*

The other way to begin is with the effect. You start with what has been impacted (effect) and then build up evidence to support an idea, argument, or premise about why (cause). The question becomes *why did this happen?*

Starting with a cause, here's an outline for a possible report in a consumer medical newsletter.

Example: Stem cells show vulnerability

- For unknown reasons, a complex single cell reverts to a simple stem cell (cause).
- Reverted stem cell is vulnerable—cancer inserts itself in cell (effect).
- Cancer genes take over (effect).
- Cancer grows, sarcoma matures (effect).
- Cell overwhelmed (effect).
- Triggers for reversion must be studied (conclusion).

2. Chronological

Much of what we write is in chronological order. For example, time rules the notes of a meeting, or an explanation of how something happened. You answer the question, *In what sequence did this happen?*

But working with chronology doesn't mean you've always got to stick to a straight, linear story. You can jump around, like Dr. Who in his Tardis. For instance, in a profile of a company, you might start in the present, jump back to the past, forward to the future, and end at the top of the arc back in the present. The important point is to make sure the time shifts happen logically. Like Dr. Who (mostly), you need to leap backward or forward for a reason. Here's a brief outline that could be a report for a nonprofit trade magazine.

Example: The widening influence of a nonprofit birthing center

- 1982—Founder of center trained as nurse midwife
- 1983—Founder recognizes need for birthing centers.
- 1990—Opened doors. Difficult—no one would come to the center.
- 1991—Introduced innovative service idea—offered home after-care visits.
- 1991–1995—Word of mouth spread—clientele increased.
- 1998–2006—More independent centers built.
- 2006–present—Working with hospitals for seamless care for mothers and babies.

3. Classification/Division

With this structure, you have a single subject that you divide into categories. You can put all the information that is the same in one section. Within the section, you can also make more divisions. Repeat the pattern until the whole subject is covered. When you need to round up information from a wide variety of sources, classifying and dividing will help you sort it out. Here's a brief writing outline for a travel website.

Example: Food truck reviews in a certain city

- Overview of how you will present the information.
- Identify an area of city.
- Within the area, sort by price, cheapest to most expensive.
- Identify next city area.
- Within the second area, sort by price, cheapest to most expensive.
- Etc.

4. Compare/Contrast

When you want to discuss the similarities and differences between things, people, places, or events, this is the structure for you. Whether you're simply looking at various options or judging which is preferable, you can use this structure in two ways.

Your first option is to start by noting everything that's similar, and then move on to the differences. At the top of the arc, you might reach a conclusion regarding the issue. Or not. You might simply be reporting the facts as you see them. Or you could also end by asking for other people's opinions.

Your second option is to move back and forth on the pros and cons, showing strengths and weaknesses as you go along. At the end of your piece, you can evaluate which side won, perhaps even giving a score. Or at the top of the arc, you might add a call to action. Here's an outline that mixes pros with cons for a business blog.

Example: Should tech companies allow journalists unfettered access to the inside workings of their company?

- **Pro:** Yes. This will result in free media attention for the company.
- **Con:** No. Because companies have no control over the specific stories the journalist will choose to tell.
- **Pro:** Yes. Companies can build their public reputation through radical transparency.
- **Con:** No. Sensitive information can be leaked that could hurt your bottom line.

5. Descriptive

The descriptive structure is like an introductory handshake—it allows you to explain your subject to anyone who's unfamiliar with it. Whether it's a place, a process, a person, or an object, your description answers all the who, what, where, when, why, and how questions. With that information, you choose how you climb the arc—*Put it in order of importance? In order of use? In order of chronology?*—and conclude with the reason your audience needs to possess this knowledge.

Here's a feasibility presentation about why the Ardèche region of France should be considered as a possible site for a company's hotel chain expansion.

Example: Is the Ardèche a good location for our hotel expansion?

- Introduction to current situation—hotel looking to expand into location that meets primary identified needs.
- The Ardèche has plenty of nature activities for tourists—hiking, biking, canoeing, etc.
- Natural attractions in the preservation area/caves, etc.
- High unemployment—good staffing possibilities.
- Weather—rain in spring and fall but little in summer.
- Major rivers already have upscale boating clientele.
- Conclusion—building here is a good possibility.

Cheat Sheet: Uses for the Structures

This list is far from definitive. These are simply suggestions to jog your imagination.

In addition, many kinds of writing could fit into more than one structure. For example, a marketing strategy document could fall under description, chronology, problem/solution, inverted pyramid, sequential, or a combination. This list is a starting place to plug in your good ideas.

- **Cause/Effect:** Opinion pieces, informative reports, histories, academic writing, persuasive arguments, evaluations, observations, social commentary
- **Chronological:** Histories, profiles, marketing strategies, business plans, obituaries
- **Classification/Division:** Product reviews, company blog posts, guides, advice columns, proposals, marketing plans
- **Compare/Contrast:** Proposals, marketing strategies, performance reports, product reviews, trade reviews, persuasive arguments, mapping future company plans, academic papers, opinion/editorials, marketing and sales strategies

- **Descriptive:** Sales, marketing, new product/program research, travel presentations, histories, research explanations, process review
- **Inverted Pyramid:** News items, press releases, newsletters, memos, pitch letters, emails
- **List/Number:** Blog posts, humorous writing, opinion pieces
- **Problem/Solution:** Company presentations, research writing, sales and marketing, evaluations, proposals, blog posts, website content creation, service information, how-to pieces
- **Question/Answer:** Informational round-ups, reports, profiles
- **Sequential:** Handbooks, manuals, marketing plans, how-to pieces, sales presentations, guides, DIY instructions

6. Inverted Pyramid

When you need to start with your most vital information first, use the inverted pyramid. This is the classic form of a newspaper story and most emails. This is also the only structure that does not follow the arc pattern.

Picture the words of a news story projected onto the form of a pyramid standing on its point. (That's a bit tricky for a pyramid, I admit—maybe you could envision the point stuck in the sand.) The most significant information appears on the widest part of the pyramid. Everything that follows would be less important and take up less space, right down to the point.

Inverted pyramid writing snags the reader with the most relevant facts first. And it's easy to cut. Back in the day, when the news was laid out in typeface, if another story broke, or the newspaper received more advertising, the existing writing could be chopped out to make room for it—from the bottom up—knowing that last paragraphs written were the most dispensable.

In this structure, you answer all the who, what, why, where, when, and how questions. You decide what's most essential and start with that. At the end, the writing has no wrap-up summary—it simply stops with the least significant point. Here's an outline for a report to a business news website.

Example: More Americans pay to join the club

- The number of Americans using Amazon Prime is rising.
- According to Consumer Intelligence Research, one in six Americans buys Amazon Prime.
- That's a 35% hike over the previous year.
- Half of Amazon's customers pay for Prime.
- That's almost as many people as those with Costco memberships.

7. List/Number

This familiar structure, also known as a "listicle," organizes information by listing a series of people, places, or things. Often used with numbering, you've seen those ubiquitous magazine articles and blog posts—*Ten Things You Never Knew About....* If you have a single subject, you can number the information, itemizing in order of importance, complexity, or silliness. For example, if it's a humorous piece, the best joke appears at the top of the arc. List/number articles tend to be easy to organize and write, even for reluctant writers. Here's one from a career website.

Example: Seven jobs for outdoor people, ranked from lowest to highest paid

- Dog walker.
- Artisanal farmer.
- Eco-tour leader.
- Outdoor recreation guide.
- Vineyard manager.
- Forest service ranger.
- Landscape architect.

8. Problem/Solution

This structure is powerful for engaging readers who need a problem solved. It's a subset of cause/effect, with the focus on fixing an issue.

The writing asks the question, *What will resolve this situation?* The problem drives everything that follows. It also takes on the form of a mystery: *How will this problem be fixed?* Even if you talk about attempts that failed, readers know you will eventually tell them about what succeeded. Identify the problem, talk about the struggle, and scale the arc to a resolution. Here's a project presentation for a company that franchises its products.

Example: Why we need a new manual

- Problem: The manual for creating franchisee websites is full of conflicting information.
- Three examples where it doesn't work.
- Solution 1: Create a simpler design.
- Solution 2: Reorganize the information.
- Solution 3: Designate a trouble-shooter.
- Conclusion: Call for action items/decision possibilities.

9. Question/Answer

Commonly called Q&A, this is a structure where you pose the questions and someone else does all the talking. Simple, right?

It seems easy, but the pitfall of Q&A is that the whole piece remains flat. First you've got a question—then a chunk of answer. Question—chunk. Question—chunk. Boring. Unless the interviewee is famous—and then everyone hangs onto whatever they say—the best way to make this structure successful is to concentrate on questions that raise tension as they progress up the arc. The questions do the work. They control the shape and pace of the writing. They have logical movement from one idea to another. They might travel up the arc in order of importance, complexity, or emotional weight.

Prepare your questions with the arc in mind. After the interview, you could shift the blocks of question/answers around to create more rising interest as long as you don't change the meaning of the person's state-ments. Whether you mention that the Q&A is edited depends on the demands of your publication.

In the interview, you should also be prepared to improvise with follow-up questions when the person throws out a new nugget of informa-tion you hadn't thought about.

Here's a Q&A outline that could appear in an investor's newsletter.

Example: A successful entrepreneur looks at the future with questions sequenced in chronological order

- What gave you the courage to start your first venture 10 years ago?
- What makes for a great startup idea in today's market?
- What advice do you have for other entrepreneurs who are looking for outside investors?
- What are your predictions about how the business world is going to evolve?
- What are you most worried about?
- What gives you hope for the future?

10. Sequential

If you need to write about a step-by-step process, sequential is your struc-ture. Recipes are a perfect example of sequential writing. Information is rolled out as the reader needs to pick it up. Many how-to pieces follow this sequence too, rising up the arc to end with the finished project.

This is tight, directive writing. Take out anything else that doesn't contribute to exactly how the reader accomplishes the goal. This is the place for bullets and plenty of strong verbs.

Let's say you run the blog of a company that sells nonrusting steel products. You're writing a content marketing article about building a DIY chicken coop. Here's the outline.

Example: How to build a critter-proof chicken coop

- Step 1. Gather materials.
- Step 2. Pour foundation.
- Step 3. Build framing walls.
- Step 4. Construct shed roof.
- Step 5. Install heavy-gauge steel mesh for all vents.
- Step 6. Stuff nonrusting steel wool into every joint.
- Step 7. Finish doors/windows/interior furnishings.
- Conclusion: Invite the girls in.

Wind Up the Pitch

A Pitch for All Reasons

Even though they're not journalists, many reluctant writers end up in a tough spot where they must pitch an article idea to an editor. You might need to write about a topic in your field to position yourself as an industry leader. Or your small company has a new product and you want to share it through a guest post on a popular blog. Whatever the situation, pitching is its own special art.

If you're facing the prospect of a pitch—by email or snail mail—here's a three-paragraph structure that will raise your chances of getting in the game. These three paragraphs give editors what they need to know to make a quick decision.

One more note: If you're writing multiple pitches, don't worry that your structure stays the same. I've used this pitch structure again and again with the same editors. No one has ever said, "Say, do you know your pitch is always the same?" As long as you have a well-aimed idea that meets the needs of the person you're pitching, the bones of your query are not a problem.

Introduction

You'll need to include a brief line of introduction. After writing a salutation, add one sentence about why you're making this pitch. This could range from a personal connection—*we spoke on the phone last week*—to an explanation of why your piece is well suited to their publication—*because you frequently cover business acquisitions, this could be a good fit for your readers.*

Paragraph 1: The Hook

This first paragraph is your grabber. Although you're pitching to the editor, this section should be aimed directly at the reader. It's written like the opening of your article—including a strong pointer sentence, three or four follow-up ideas, and an ending question or summation of the whole piece. You want to mimic the style and tone of the publication.

Here's an example for Atlantic.com that writer Sophia McDonald Bennett has been kind enough to share:

> *There's bad news/good news on the tech front. A report from the Silicon Valley Competitiveness and Innovation Project says entrepreneurs are thinking twice before moving to the San Francisco Bay Area. High housing costs and long commutes are two factors. But that's good news for small and medium-sized towns across the globe looking to cash in on the high-tech boom. Miniature metropolises that attract tech firms share three commonalities: a relatively low cost of living, universities able to train a skilled workforce, and infrastructure, such as business incubators. What lessons can other communities learn from them?*

Paragraph 2: The Pay-Off

This paragraph tells what you will deliver. Now there's a shift in tone. You're all business. You talk straight to the editor. You include your idea for the title and any subhead. It might get changed later, but it allows you to explain in fewer words. You can suggest a length for the piece (unless it's for a section of the publication where the word count never changes—in that case, leave it out). You also point toward the category—it might be for a blog post, a column, or a feature. Finish this section with the summary of what this piece will do.

Here's the template for the first sentence in the pay-off paragraph. It fits in the most important information. I've never found a way to shorten it, but if you figure out how, please share it with me.

In my _____ (insert number)-word _____ (category), "_____" (title and subhead), I will _____ (dynamic verb) _____ (summary).

If you have trouble ending that sentence, ask yourself, "What will my readers have that they don't have now?" That's the pay-off.

After that first long sentence, describe how you will deliver it. In no more than three or four other sentences, give the editor the bones of the piece. You may offer more details about your subject. You might bullet three of the main topics you'll cover. You can also include any important sources, sidebars, and, if applicable, photo availability.

Here's Sophia's second paragraph:

In my 1,200-word feature, "Lessons from Small Communities Winning Big in the High Tech Boom," I'll share the advice from three small and medium-sized towns with established or growing technology clusters. I'll interview Andrew Hyde with Ignite Boulder and Startup Weekend in Boulder, Colorado; Simon Bond with SETSquared in Bristol, England; and Kadri Koivik with Garage48 HUB in Tartu, Estonia. I will explain how these communities managed to attract hot high-tech startups despite their lack of major urban name recognition.

The second-paragraph template tests your ideas. I realize that in many cases, you're just imagining an idea. You're taking an amorphous concept out of the air and trying to shove it into a firm format. However, when you attempt to meet the demands of the template, you see exactly where your thoughts are still unformed or unfocused. You might change the slant. You could tweak it. Or throw it up in the air and let it come down differently. Stuffing it into this template saves time, because you don't have to write a whole draft to see what works.

Paragraph 3: The Connection

Here's where you say why you should write this rather than anyone else. Put your credentials on the table. List where your work has appeared. In an email, put in links to any place where editors could sample your writing, even if it's just the company website.

If you don't have writing credentials, you have your job—which is why you're pitching in the first place. Mention specific knowledge the job confers on you. You could also note your education if that gives you more credibility in your field. As a freelancer, Sophia included her own website. You'd stick to your company or business contact information.

> My work has appeared on over two dozen websites and magazines including _TheAtlantic.com_, _Institute for Local Self-Reliance_, _RecycleNation_, _Sip Northwest_, _Oregon Business_, and _1859 Oregon's Magazine_. You can view additional clips and find out more about me at _www.sophiathewriter.com_.

Short and Sharp Gets the Job Done

Try to keep your paragraphs as tight as possible. After you've written a first draft, go back and cut anything extraneous. Ideally, each paragraph will fit in the email window without a lot of scrolling.

Plan at least two other places to pitch, so if or when the rejection comes—or it's all silence—you can send it out again.

Structures You Can Build On

If you're the kind of reluctant writer who's always felt constrained when following a pattern, I'm hoping that at least one of the structures offered here will help you. Frameworks come with a lot of benefits.

For one, they can save you time and effort because they take the guesswork out of your writing process. A framework also allows you to break your writing down into less intimidating pieces. After all, it's great to know you only have to write a couple of sentences for a chunk, right? And those chunks can build. Your writing will gain both clarity of thought and form.

I'm also hoping that by becoming more aware of structures, you'll start to notice other ones that aren't covered here. The world of words is full of writing patterns. Just grab one and hang on.

Write On Exercise: Plot Three Ways

Time: Ten minutes

Similar to the exercise in Chapter 4, this writing practice gives you a chance to try out different structures. You'll need 3" x 5" cards and several sheets of paper.

Step 1. Decide on the subject. Take something you have to write—anything, from an overdue thank-you note to the annual report. If it's long, you'll work with the beginning only.

Step 2. Write on your cards. Put one fact, one piece of information, whatever you want to say, on each card. Keep it short.

Step 3. Draw an arc. This will work for nine of your options. If you want to start with the inverted pyramid, draw that instead.

Step 4. Write the subject underneath.

Step 5. Choose a structure. You have been given ten basic frameworks. Write your choice under the subject.

Step 6. Place your cards. The cards will be ordered depending on which structure you're using.

Step 7. Repeat the process. Make another arc or pyramid. Choose a different structure and place the cards again.

As you go through this exercise, notice how different structures change the order of your cards.

The subject and the formats don't have to be a good fit. In fact, try some that are silly. For instance, for a thank-you note, try the inverted pyramid. What's the most important thing you want to say about Aunt Neva's gift? What's the least? Or use the listicle—"Five reasons Aunt Neva's gift won't be forgotten." Come up with quick answers and you may discover ideas that could be included in a sincere note.

Or maybe Aunt Neva has a sense of humor and would like your listicle.

This exercise is useful when you're stuck. It allows you to play with your information. If you always write a certain way, it can show you other options. Use it to fine-tune your writing to the structure you need.

Real-World Review: A Hated Structure Turns Out to Be Gold

I first discovered the value of structures when I was at college in the late 1960s—a.k.a. the days when dinosaurs roamed the earth.

My all-women's school (now co-ed Chatham University in Pittsburgh, Pennsylvania) had a required course called "The Arts." The scope was ridiculously ambitious. In three semesters it was meant to cover all artistic endeavors throughout the entire Western Civilization—starting chronologically with cave paintings and galloping on into the 20th century.

The workload was massive. The goal was to successfully identify hundreds of famous works of art. Tests consisted of slides flashing by or needle drops onto records for passages of music. It was easy to screw up. For instance, William Turner, (1775–1851) was not considered an impressionist.

Oh well, he should have been.

Besides all that mad memorization, students also had to go out into Pittsburgh five times each semester—fifteen excursions altogether—and attend arts events. It could be theater, dance, gallery openings, whatever. And for each, we had to turn in what were called "Arts Cards." They weren't cards. They were 500- to 750-word reviews, based on a specific four-question structure. At first I struggled to write to the form. But after a while, I cranked them out.

I hated it on two levels. The first complaint was about the frantic pace. Fascinating works of art ran by with no opportunity to actually delve into them. Second, my arts education was the classic "mile wide and an inch deep." Yes, I did know the difference between, as we joked, "the Bauhaus and the doghouse." I wouldn't embarrass myself at a dinner party. But my knowledge ended after two sentences into any subject.

Mine was one of the vociferous voices challenging the curriculum. And a few years later, in the tumult of the early 1970s, "The Arts" course was abandoned.

And yet, after all these years, one aspect of that most hated course has proved to be useful: the Arts Card structure. Any time I needed to review anything, I had it. Fast.

So now I'm giving that structure to you. These are the exact four questions for an Arts Card—I've never forgotten them. They can be extended way beyond the arts to include reviewing a product, a process, a software program—anything you need to examine thoughtfully.

- **What was the maker/designer/author/choreographer/artist trying to do?**
  Here's where you sum up the overarching theme or goal of the work. This is big-picture stuff. Whether it was created by an individual or a team, you're looking at the impulse that brought the work into being. What were they delving into?
- **How did they go about doing it?**
  This entails a description focused on *how* they accomplished what they were trying to do. If the artwork has a plot, no matter how engrossing, don't be tempted to outline it here. This will save you from ever having to write "spoiler alert." If you're describing a process or a product, this question makes it easy to relate how and why it was created.
- **Did they succeed?**
  This is a terrific question. It's at the heart of the review. Perhaps they succeeded in one area, but failed in another. You get to decide. You explain why and support your opinion based on the answers to the first two questions.
- **So what?**
  Here's where you tie your observations to the greater context or the bigger world. You answer the questions of how or why this work is relevant. Why does it deserve notice? How does it solve problems? What difference does it make?

There you have it. That long-gone Arts Card structure still lives. I hope it comes in handy if someone calls upon you to review anything in your field.

CHAPTER 7

Constructing the Personal Essay

Writing Problem: *I need to tell a story from my point of view.*

Rx: *Use the personal essay structure—yes, there is one.*

The personal essay is a workhorse. It can be trotted out for all kinds of writing situations—op-eds, blog posts, college applications, speeches. Because this particular kind of essay is so useful for so many things, it deserves its own chapter.

First we'll look at what sets the personal essay apart from all others. Then we'll examine the difference between telling and showing. I'll give you a simple personal essay structure you can use again and again. After that, we'll look at the building blocks of nonfiction scenes—like time, place, character, and description.

Plus, we've got **Cheat Sheet: What's the News? What's the Story?**, with a comparison between showing and telling. **Write On Exercise: Scenes and CSD** focuses on concrete sensory details you might overlook.

We'll also deconstruct a sample essay in **Bad Light**. And to top it off, there's a **Real-World Review: Michel de Montaigne's Dusty Mantle** about the invention of the personal essay—hint: this form's been around longer than you might think.

What's So Personal About the Personal Essay?

If you read Chapter 6, you know that essays can share an opinion, an idea, or a persuasive argument. They can also be written in the first-person—but that alone doesn't mean it's a personal essay. On the most basic level, the difference between personal essays and others hinges on one defining feature: whether or not there's a shift in the writer's point of view.

In most contemporary essays, the writer's perspective remains the same from beginning to end. If you have to write a piece, "Five Reasons to Use Our Company's App," your position on the subject doesn't change. Even if the material concludes in an unexpected way, or you add your own ideas to the mix—your stance on the topic remains the same. It's static.

However, in the personal essay (and good memoirs) there's a shift in the writer's perspective between the beginning and the end. By the time you've climbed the arc, you, the writer—along with the reader—now see things a little differently. This doesn't have to be a major, earth-shattering epiphany. It could be a quiet aha moment. It could focus on an idea or feeling unnoticed before. Something subtle. But big or small, the writer's point of view changes. That alteration in perspective is what separates personal essay writing from everything else. You move.

A personal essay is also defined by what it is not. It's not a rant—no shift in perspective there. It's not an exposé. It's not a confessional, no matter how intense. It's not a purposeless swab through the writer's brain, revealing details that were best left in the dark, no matter how much the writer self-justifies. Sure, you can write (and read) that stuff. Be my guest. But by my lights, it doesn't reveal and resonate the way a personal essay does.

Three Parts Make a Whole

Personal essays have a basic three-part structure—certainty, confusion/chaos, and change.

Start with Certainty

At the beginning—whether you're describing a scene, or developing an idea—there's a sense of certainty. The writer knows something—or perhaps, doesn't know something—but it's *for sure*. It's just the way things are. One term for this is "unearned certainty," a phrase I first heard in a writing class taught by an amazing teacher and author, Debra Gwartney.

Often this certainty has an emotional quality that doesn't come from direct personal experience. For example:

My mother always said...

Or they might simply be describing something the way it's always been.

The bucket's rope was wrapped around the windlass.

Or, the unearned certainty comes from the sure idea of known repetition.

That Sunday started out the same as all the other Sundays.

As readers, we pick up on these opening clues. In good storytelling, they will pay off. The writer is going to get knocked off that position of certainty by an experience. We know that the writer's mother is probably going to be wrong. Or something's up with that bucket and rope. Or the Sunday is going to go south at any moment. It's our hook, and we're happy to take it.

Move to Confusion/Chaos

As the essay progresses up the narrative arc, something happens. In screenplays, this is the inciting incident—it's the thing that kicks things off. And often whatever is happening gets worse, or more complicated, or more important. This is the heart of the story and the action often moves right into confusion, or even chaos.

Settled ideas are thrown out the window.

Turns out my new husband hated waiting for me to try on outfits.

The stakes get higher as the essay climbs.

My father couldn't remember the list the doctor asked him to repeat. I wanted to shout, "It's monkey, apple, badger!"

Make a Shift

Near the end, the perception changes. An awareness arises. There's a new connection to the wider world. Because this shift can lead in countless directions, the endings take many forms.

You shouldn't introduce a totally new thought—sometimes called a *bomb*—that has no relation to the previous writing. But you don't have to neatly tie it up in a bow, either. A realization may occur, but personal essays don't have to resolve.

For instance, in this example the closing thought connects to a new unsettled view:

I'm leaving everything I know so I can know much more.

Sometimes the promise in the beginning appears at the end, like a snake biting its tail. Readers delight in finding those connections—especially if they don't see them coming. (Think of the endings of the best Garrison Keillor "Lake Wobegone" stories, tying back to a beginning he appeared to abandon long before.) However, the tail is not the head. The ending is not reiterating the beginning. Or else, why bother reading the piece? When you return to the opening promise, the writer (and the reader) now see it from a slightly altered point of view. In this essay that opens with fears about her competitive mother-in-law, the final line reads:

Finally, the sweat broke across my forehead and I smiled up at her. We sat down for our picnic.

Or perhaps the essay ends with what author Adam Gropnik calls "a left turn into traffic." It carries a certain surprise, or makes a connection that is odd-lot or unusual. Perhaps it might end like this:

Some people treat their weekends like fine china. Others would rather use paper plates.

Tell vs. Show

That three-step structure will get you started. But it won't guarantee that you've got an interesting essay on your hands. Why? Sometimes writers hold the reader at an arm's length away from the action; even as they *tell* them about what happened they don't *show* them. The reader can't get inside the story. By telling, the writer never fulfills the implied promise of a personal essay—*let me take you with me and show how things changed.* Even if the material builds, it's boring.

To bring the reader with you on the journey you can employ the old writing adage: "Show, don't tell." Let's define what that means.

Telling has its important place. As a reluctant writer, most of what you do is telling, because telling is exposition. It rolls out the information. Whether the facts are ordinary or life-and-death, you're still conveying the actualities, processes, or opinions about a subject to your reader. From marketing reports to business memos, plenty of writing needs that exact kind of telling. With telling, you may use quotes from people. You may talk about situations. You might even describe a story. But your writing carries a certain dispassion:

Within a three-day time period, we raised $300,000.

With *showing*, the reader gets inside the story because you take them through scenes that involve protagonists, dialogue, and concrete sensory details. Showing has conflict, drama. It's not that you ignore data, processes, or opinions, but now you hook the reader with some kind of emotional exploration or promise and deliver it by the end:

Looking around the room at my colleagues' grinning, exhausted faces, I couldn't believe what we'd just pulled off: $300,000 raised in just three days.

See the difference?

Make a Scene: The Elements

Instead of reporting, put the action into a real-life scene—or into a shortened version I call a *scenelet*. It's one of the best ways to grab a reader's attention. So what constitutes a scene?

Cheat Sheet: What's the News? What's the Story?

The differences between telling (news) and showing (story)

News	Story
Conflict—reported as news	Conflict—told through a narrative with scenes, etc.
Hook—most important facts	
Structure—inverted pyramid	Hook—inciting incident
Fact delivery—order of importance	Structure—story arc
	Fact delivery—rising action
People—sources	People—protagonists/characters
Quotes	
Neutral voice	Dialogue
	Personal perspective/point of view

Scenes Are Grounded in Time and Space

"Grounded in time and space" is another quote I first learned from Debra Gwartney. Readers need to know where they are. It doesn't have to be the first thing you say, but don't wait too long. Otherwise your reader will feel like they're in a balloon, hovering above the action, not sure where or how to get in.

For example, situating the reader can be simple:

When I was young we lived in Ohio.

Or specific:

Last week on a country road, the late afternoon sun glinted on the railroad crossing arms lowering in front of my car.

Scenes Have Beginnings, Middles, and Endings

Each scene has its own arc—with a beginning, middle, and end. The bulk of a scene is in the rising action of the middle. Beginnings and ending are trickier—you want to keep them as short as you can. So ask yourself, how late into the action can I launch and how quickly can I exit the scene? This gives immediacy and vitality.

Scenes Have Concrete Sensory Details

Often abbreviated as CSD, concrete sensory details are what you can hear, taste, touch, feel, and experience. The sensation of time elapsing also falls into this category.

If you're writing a scene at a track meet, think back on all that you came across. For example:

the sun-heated bench under your thighs

the cadence of footfalls

the javelin's thunk

the dry protein bar on your tongue

a flag crackling in the wind

the slow-motion boredom between events

Of course, not all sensory details work equally well in a piece. For a scene's first draft, you might stuff as many as you can in there. Then pick and choose which details support your cable-car sentence (Chapter 3) and remove the rest.

Scenes Have Immediacy

If you want readers to get up close and personal, get rid of the filter on your consciousness—you. Remove *I saw, I heard, I thought,* and even *I felt.* Substitute vivid action pictures.

For instance, instead of:

I felt nauseated.

Change to something more vivid:

My meal insisted it would rather return to my mouth.

Rather than:

I knew the cookies were underdone.

Try stating what you see:

The cookies crumbled into floury bits.

That said, there are times when you might choose to give your reader some distance, especially if your scene is emotionally challenging. You can filter what readers experience with *I saw, I heard, I felt*, and so on.

Five yards from the overturned car, I saw the back wheels spinning high above the pavement. I heard the grinding of their final revolutions.

Scenes Show a Variety of Frames

The facts in a scene are shaped by the writer's highly subjective point of view. Like a camera, the writer can show us a wide frame, medium frame, and close-ups.

Wide frames establish where the action takes place:

We stopped our horses in a field of daisies, spreading out in waves before us.

Medium frames move in, often showing relationships:

Our leader glared at us dudes from under his cowboy hat. He spat at a daisy by his horse's foot, neatly knocking it sideways.

Close-up frames deal with specifics and reactions:

A hapless bee tumbled off the daisy's white petals, its wings glinting in the sunlight.

And please note, in an essay written in first-person, the one thing you can't do is get inside someone else's head. You can't say what another person is thinking. You could guess. But you'd have to tell us that. Just like in real life, you can't actually go inside. The wide, medium, and close-up shots are all you've got.

Scenes Have Protagonists/Characters

In reporting, you deal with people as sources. In a scene, you, and those around you, act as characters. And you're the main protagonist. Even if you devote an entire essay to another person, it's still about you. You're telling the story. The shift in point of view is yours—although another person may also be shifting. Bottom line: it's your essay.

Sometimes you have to cut people out, even when in real life they were there. That happens when those characters don't support the point of the story. A student of mine wrote a funny essay about how his family visited a famous theme park and inadvertently found themselves in a deserted back lot. The writer's little sister was crushed to discover a woman, dressed as one of her favorite animated princesses, mashing it up with a pirate. That incident was witnessed by several more of the writer's siblings. But they never appeared in the story because they had nothing to contribute.

Scenes Have Dialogue

In reporting or telling, you track down specific quotes and use them to illuminate the information. In scenes, people have conversations. You can use dialogue to move the action or as a shortcut for description.

Often, what someone says reveals a great deal about them.

"You know," my aunt says, peering down at my faded running shoes, "your legs would look so much better if you wore heels."

We know she's sharp-eyed, judgmental, and offers her opinions too freely. None of which you have to say. She says it for you.

The trick here is to remember what people said with accuracy. A debate rages among memoir writers about remembered dialogue—how could anyone recall pages of dialogue they heard as a child? I fall into the camp that says, as long as you make it clear that this is what you remember, then that's your memory. Although, I'd also suggest keeping dialogue short, so it doesn't strain credulity.

However, don't invent. Anything. If you can't remember, say so. I believe the universe provides nonfiction writers with everything they need—and more. In fact, sometimes you have to cut back because the raw truth sounds like fiction.

Let's say the story isn't coming out the way you think it should. What if you're tempted to twist it a bit to make it fit your idea? Please don't. Instead, go back and reexamine what you've been given. There's a reason you want to tell this. Powerful truths are embedded in the facts. They're like puzzle pieces. You may need to assemble them differently. A better story may be under your nose but you haven't noticed it yet. In 14 years of university teaching, I never saw an essay made worse by sticking to the truth. And most writing comes alive when the real story is discovered. The truth rings through.

Scenes Have Rising Stakes—Wins and Losses

In a scene, tension comes from conflict. The characters bang into each other with differences of opinions, or desires, or motivations. Sometimes, outside influences cross the protagonist—such as weather or illness. As a result, characters win or lose, or they win in the end and almost lose in the middle. Many writers—not just reluctant ones—want to avoid conflict at all cost. They hate it.

But characters need to struggle. The last thing you want in a scene is smoothness:

We went for a walk. It was a beautiful day. We were happy.

Keep score of the conflict. This score keeping may not appear in the writing, but it's important that you know who's winning and who's losing. And why. This is part of your storytelling.

By keeping score, you will also see whether or not you're an active player in the drama—you should be. If your essay is all about the terrible things that have happened to you—but you play no part and are simply the victim—you give the reader no place to go inside the story. Except to pity you. It's just a sob story. You have to have some agency to arrive at a shift in your point of view.

Scenes Have Emotional Stand-Ins

We live in a material world. Often, in modern essays, physical things act as stand-ins for emotions. Instead of telling about feelings—or worse yet, crying (it's usually better to let the readers cry than the characters)—you can show emotions with a description of a substitute object.

For instance, at a funeral gathering, a timeworn dining table dominates the room. Without saying so, the description of the table stands in for the writer's feelings about the newly departed grandmother whose drive for control (or cleanliness) still lingers.

The table crowded the dining room, its surface scrubbed to a matte finish by my grandmother's relentless cleaning. Nobody wanted it.

Or perhaps a gift one character gives another stands in for the emotion behind it. An uncommunicative soldier presents a service patch to his daughter that commemorates his time in Iraq. The vast gulf between them is bridged for a moment. The patch stands in for the unsaid, "I'm sorry I wasn't there when you needed me."

Sometimes the essay centers on the material stand-in. It might be a story about a house, built for the local people in an foreign country, but left behind unfinished when the writer returns home. Why didn't it get finished? That house represents all the unspoken cultural misunderstandings between good-hearted people who care about each other.

Scenes Have Visual Descriptions

Whether you're capturing someone's bushy eyebrows or the telling details of your own surroundings, you are describing what you're seeing. You're sharing the images you see on the movie screen in your mind.

Sometimes reluctant writers shy away from any description at all, which makes it harder for the reader to see it on their own movie screen. Try to find a telling detail that is a fresh observation, not just a tired been-there-seen-that phrase.

Compress a Scene with a Scenelet

Especially when writing a short, short essay—under 500 words—you don't have the luxury to build a whole scene. So you can compress it down with a *scenelet*. Scenelets contain only a few of the elements. You grab just one or two to get the reader inside the action and call it good.

It can be as simple as

One afternoon in the coffee shop....

There you are. Readers can picture a coffee shop.

You could add more elements as needed. If this coffee shop has particular important details—and if they really happened—you can slide those in. Maybe someone just gave you bad news (dialogue) in the coffee shop. Perhaps you'd use a description about how your fingers felt making patterns in the spilled sugar on the counter (CSD). That action could also be a physical stand-in for the confusion you're feeling.

The beauty of a scenelet is that you give readers an idea and plenty of room to fill in their own details.

Checklist: Elements of a Scene

All scenes will have these elements. Scenelets may only have a few.

- ☐ Time
- ☐ Location
- ☐ Rising action
- ☐ Beginning, middle, and end
- ☐ Protagonists/characters
- ☐ Dialogue
- ☐ Conflict
- ☐ Wins and losses
- ☐ Concrete sensory detail (CSD)
- ☐ Frames—Wide shots, medium shots, and close-ups
- ☐ Descriptions
- ☐ Substitutes—material world for inner feelings

Insert Exposition Here

The best time to put in descriptions, a backstory, or important facts is the moment when the reader needs them in order to stay involved. It's handled many ways, but here are two basic techniques.

Weave Exposition Into the Narrative

The first method is to insert facts into the action. These facts may be a description that clarifies what has been set up. Here's the beginning of a scene:

> *The TSA delegates stood around the hotel ballroom, dressed in gray slacks, blue blazers, and fire-engine-red ties.*

But these people have nothing to do with airline safety. So the next piece of information has to be about defining that TSA acronym. In this case, the writer tells us, it stands for the *Technology Students Association*. Once that's established, the scene can go forward into dialogue.

Or perhaps readers need to know a backstory in order to understand where the scene is headed. In an essay about a loving grandfather, it's important to realize he wasn't always that way. The writer could start off

Write On Exercise: Scenes and CSD

Time: Ten minutes

This practice exercise tunes you into the sensory world around you. And it's fun to do.

Step 1. Choose a spot. Take yourself to a familiar place with people—coffee shop, park bench, wherever you choose.

Step 2. Free-write CSD. (5 minutes) Make a list of all the sensory information that's coming at you—everything. Keep going until the time is up.

Step 3. Write in scene. (5 minutes) Now write the beginning of a real-life scene, reporting what you're observing. Use the scene elements from the cheat sheet and at least some of the concrete sensory details you just experienced.

Step 4. Review. Notice what the CSD adds to the story. How is your writing different?

---

in scene, and then weave in a fact from her grandfather's own neglected childhood:

Grandpa was one of 10 kids, born to a father who terrified them all.

Later, inside a scene that shows the caring relationship with his granddaughter, the writer could throw in a fact for contrast:

I never heard him tell my grandmother he loved her.

Break the Narrative

A broken narrative is classic in feature writing for magazines and newspapers, and well suited for personal essays. The structure starts in scene, and then breaks away—ideally at a cliffhanger moment—and takes up a chunk of exposition that we need to know. It could be a backstory that led up to the scene. Then we move back into scene—usually some time has passed, but not always—and the action builds again. Then the narrative breaks away on another point of tension. More exposition. It might be projections for the future, or an explanation of why the action in scene is going that way. At the top of the arc, we return to scene one last time, where there may or may not be resolution. Three scenes and two break-aways is about what you can fit into a short essay, but as long as you keep climbing the arc, the number of them is up to you.

As an example of the broken narrative, here's the outline of a charming short essay, written by Bonnie Shelton, now well into her career as a multi-media journalist. She wrote this when she was a freshman in my university class. Her narrator speaks with two voices—her childhood self in scene, and her grownup self looking back on the action. She has three scenelets and two breaks.

Starts in scene—second grade classroom—a child's point of view.

On her desk, she finds a crumpled up love note from a fellow second grader.

She is appalled.

Breaks narrative—jumps out of scene to explain why—a grownup point of view.

She was worried about being teased.

She was embarrassed by his interest.

Her upbringing made her think this attention might be sinful.

Back in scene—the second grade classroom.

She considers swallowing the paper, like a spy.

Settles for hiding the balled-up paper in the waste can.

Her erstwhile boyfriend discovers it.

He shows her his true offering, hidden in the paper—a 25-cent ruby ring.

Breaks narrative—jumps out of scene.

She discusses the ramifications of this most romantic gesture.

Notes that she may never again receive such a heartfelt gift.

Back in scene—second grade classroom

Her crushed would-be boyfriend pitches the ring into the waste can.

Bonnie ends with—*But at the time, all I could think was, it's a good thing I didn't try to eat that.*

With either of these exposition techniques, the final consideration is timing. You can use exposition to control the pacing of a story. Exposition, in any form, whether descriptions or facts or breakaways, keeps the pace more leisurely.

However, as the action or ideas progress, you want things to move along. Use less exposition. When the action gets hot, it's distracting, and sometimes even annoying, for a reader to be pulled away for explanations.

Deconstructing a Personal Essay

The following essay was written by Nick Bernard, a web developer at Droplr, when he was in my writing class at the University of Oregon. It plays with the reversal of the common idea that shining a light on family troubles is a way to heal them—and it follows the personal essay form.

Bad Light
Why go to the trouble of installing a skylight and then cover it up?

I usually only see my family at wedding receptions, baptisms, and funeral services.

That's the certainty—the way things always have been.

This infrequency wouldn't be uncommon for relatives separated by state lines or plane trips, but my Uncle Guy and Aunt Laurel live in a house right up the road from me. It's within walking distance. Christmas, however, is the annual vain attempt to bring our family together.

Now the reader knows this is about family unease. It raises the question—why? There's a quality of confusion starting.

Last Christmas my brother, Robert, visited from Seattle. He's actually my half-brother; my father raised him as a single dad while battling a long divorce. They're trying to restore their relationship, but even now, after twenty years, every conversation finds its way back to the pain of Robert's formative years.

This is a backstory woven in so that now we get a glimpse as to why.

My father, Robert, and I made the trek up the street to Guy and Laurel's house.

We are now grounded in time and space and moving into a scene.

The worn Astroturf on the sagging front porch welcomed us to their suburban abode. My uncle is tall and stocky with silver hair. He was wearing the only thing I ever saw him wear—a Pendleton shirt with the sleeves rolled up to his elbows, khaki slacks, and brown penny loafers. I hugged Laurel, who sported her favorite holiday sweater.

Guy gave me a firm handshake and asked if I'd pledged a frat yet. I told him I hadn't and he launched into another rant about his college days. "It didn't take me long to figure out a frat was the only way to get any girls," he said. "And beer too. Girls and beer.... I ditched those squares in the dorms and never looked back."

The telling details and uncomfortable dialogue cued by the word *rant* act as stand-ins for the unsaid uncomfortable feelings. It raises the stakes.

I am one of those squares and particularly repulsed by the frat-boy lifestyle. So I'm never really sure how to respond to his statements. But, after all, that was only one of the many aspects where our ideologies clashed. I knew I wouldn't make it through dinner without Guy hassling me to join the army.

This backstory exposition raises the emotional tension. The conflict is happening.

We all filed through the kitchen and Guy directed our attention to the newest addition to their home—a round glass skylight in the ceiling of the living room. Guy explained how it all worked. "It's not any old window," he said proudly. "They cut a hole in the roof and run a tube of highly reflective metal down to the ceiling. Lets that natural light in."

"They come in a ten- or a twelve-inch diameter," Laurel said. "But you know Guy—he had to get the bigger model."

This is character-revealing dialogue.

"Looks nice," my dad said.

"Brightens the whole room up," Robert agreed.

"Couldn't you have just bought a lamp?" I asked.

In the face of the others' polite comments, the writer gets his snarky put-down into the fray. He is ignored. This is a pause in the pace of the writing. Then the story goes up a notch.

The room was quiet for a while until Laurel broke the silence. "Well, to be honest, I wish they made some sort of shade to put over it," she admitted. "Most of the time there's too much light."

There on the floor, the pea-green shag carpet showed a faded circular patch between the coffee table and the flocked Christmas tree.

The telling details the writer inserts show a lot about his feelings for his relatives. It's also another pause. But now the problem has been introduced. The story notches again. Even though it's small, the action is moving to the top of the arc.

Guy laughed and said, "Hell, most of the time we tape a piece of black construction paper over it."

I tried to take in what it all meant. Who would go to the trouble of installing a skylight, this promise to improve their lives, and then cover it up?

The phrase, *this promise to improve their lives*, shows that the skylight is working hard as a material stand-in for the idea of a family trying to make things better in their relationships.

Everyone stared through the glorified hole in the roof to the late afternoon sky above. I studied my aunt and uncle and tried to think why we only managed to see one another twice a year. I looked at my brother Robert and wondered why I hardly knew him. I examined our father and questioned whose fault it was that the two of them had barely spoken for twenty years.

None of this was by accident. My aunt and uncle could walk down the hill to visit me. I could have phoned Robert. My dad could have called him. Somehow, the soonest I'd see Robert was the next Christmas, and it'd take Grandma dying or cousin Cate getting married to see Guy and Laurel before that.

This is a moment of realization.

I lifted my head back. My eyes squinted hard at the late sun pouring in. A small corner of black construction paper was still hanging on the edge of the glass. Guy reached up and taped a fresh sheet over the hole. "Gotta keep out the bad light," he said.

My eyes relaxed—oh, much better.

The skylight becomes the metaphor for shining a light on problems. The tiny shift is completed when the writer comes to an agreement with his family—*let's just leave things in the dark.*

The Essay Works

The personal essay can be effective in many situations. It's an appealing form because it allows you to get close to readers. Whether you use your story as an example inside a larger piece, or you have a chance to talk about your organization's mission from your point of view, look for chances to let this workhorse out of the barn.

Real-World Review: Michel de Montaigne's Dusty Mantle

You'll never forget that a personal essay contains a tiny shift in perception if you know about the huge shift that took place when the essay was invented. Yes, one person, Michel de Montaigne, sat down and created a whole new way of writing. And it happened much further back in history than you might think, given the essay's current popularity.

I first got interested in Montaigne when I read author E. B. White's "The Essayist." When he wrestles with his own writing, Mr. White says, he is cheered because there, in the back of his writing closet, hangs Michel de Montaigne's cloak, "smelling slightly of camphor." Anyone who attempts an essay owes a certain debt to Montaigne.

The facts: He was born in 1533 in Bordeaux, France, and died in 1592. At his father's insistence, he grew up speaking Latin, the language of scholars, as his mother tongue. He trained as a lawyer and held the position of mayor, but he spent most of his life writing at his estates.

He lived in tumultuous times. The astonishing shift in consciousness that was the Renaissance was covering Europe like a tsunami, a wave starting around the Mediterranean and pushing northward through the course of a hundred years. People's perceptions were changing radically.

You can see this shift by looking at the innovations that occurred in paintings. Medieval paintings portrayed odd dislocated floating floors, tiny cities, and giant baby Jesuses. It's not that the artists were blinded to natural reality. It wasn't an important attribute. Then in an historical blink of the eye, paintings transformed into representations of a more natural world. Perspective and depth of field were valued. Suddenly, flat ceilings of palaces were painted to look as though whole carved stone balconies were rising above the viewer's head. Michelangelo included images of realistic legs dangling down from the ceiling of the Sistine Chapel. New subjects—not all religious—occupied both artists and patrons.

Montaigne brought this change of consciousness to writing.

The classical and contemporary writing of his day took the formal rigid rules of rhetoric, argument, and discourse—most of it in Latin. But that wasn't what Montaigne wanted. He wanted to walk around inside his head, and examine his thoughts and feelings. He wanted to arrive at conclusions that were personal discoveries, not objective truths. He wrote, not in Latin, but in common French. He named his writing *essais*—from the French verb *to try.*

Montaigne's writing covers a wide array of topics, but most of it follows a form. He starts with a thought or an observation. He explores facets of it. Often the subjects were variations on aspects of death—not as the Church saw it, or even as philosophers did, but as he struggled to come to terms with the inevitable. By the end, nothing gets resolved, yet something is illuminated. Radical.

Montaigne's invention brought writing into the Renaissance.

Now, I understand that reluctant writers may very well want to leave Montaigne's dusty cloak hanging far, far back in the closet. But even if you never write an essay, you can get some value out of Montaigne: writing reflects its society. And in a world where communications are quickly being re-imagined as tweets, emojis, memes, gifs, and beyond, it's good to take notice of new innovations. Shift happens.

EDIT

SECTION 3 INTRODUCTION

Sebastian J. Barbarito is known for this quote: "The difference between mediocrity and excellence is attention to detail."

In writing terms, you could say that the difference between bad writing and good writing is editing. Writing once is not enough.

However, editing is a different set of skills. Whether what you're writing is as short as an email, or as long as forever, you need to allow yourself the first messy brain dump draft. Now as you re-vision it, you don't have to make it up out of whole cloth. Now you're shaping the words. If it needs more, you're filling in the gaps, stitching in necessary information. If it's too much, you're snipping, moving things around, tightening here and there until the thoughts take a writing shape.

And certain techniques and tricks make the editing process much easier. The EDIT section of the book will take you through a step-by-step series of them.

Edit From Big to Small

Chapter 8 is all about the **big-picture edit**—that moment when you sweep through your material and make high-level changes like rearranging material and gut-checking your main idea.

Chapter 9 zooms in on the **medium-focus edit** by explaining four quick editing tools that get you to a strong draft fast.

Chapter 10 gets even more detailed with **pointer sentences**—those vital summary sentences that guide readers in the right direction. If you've already got them, we'll look at how to make them better. If they're missing, we'll offer tips for constructing the clearest and most concise.

And finally, Chapter 11 gives you a close-up checklist for the **picky details** and copy edits needed for the final polish.

Okay...ready, set, edit.

CHAPTER 8

The Big-Picture Edit

Writing Problem: *How do I know what to keep and what to cut?*

Rx: *Snap your ideas into line with a long-view edit.*

There's a saying that we change hats when we move from writing to editing. The process really is different. Even if you edit at the same time as you write, you are switching back and forth, using different parts of your brain, as you jump between tasks.

However, it recently occurred to me to wonder what those two hats look like. I picture my writing hat as a homemade knitted beret, in bright colors, slouching off to one side of my head. It's messy and a bit itchy, but well worn. What would yours be? And how would it look different from your editing hat? Mine's a neatly blocked felt cloche, with a discreet dark ribbon around it—there's a lot of control in that hat.

So why bother about hats? Sometimes, a picture can actually help you define these two processes.

In this chapter, you have arrived at the moment of editing. Before, you were the communicator, bringing your thoughts into the material world.

Now you are the judgmental editor. You have my permission to act as if somebody else wrote your work.

We're going to look at **four main steps** to guide you in a sweeping overview edit, along with two **Words to the Wise**. The first, **Five Virtues Good Editors Share**, deals with qualities you can adopt for yourself. The second, **Sort Out Spaghetti Strands**, helps you sort out what to do when more than one main writing idea ends up in your first draft. The **Write On Exercise** is a redux of the all-important **Two Minutes of Heavy Lifting** from Chapter 3. In the **Real-World Review: Spaghetti Strands Provide Plenty of Material,** author Rosemarie Ostler uses the big-picture edit to pull multiple story ideas out of one swift first draft—saving time and effort.

Go Backward to Move Forward

Big-picture edits revisit four of the methods you used to create your first draft. First, we're going to look at the WIIFM (Chapter 1), to see whether it fits the chosen format or structure. Second, we'll re-examine that cable-car sentence (Chapter 3), both for the subject and the slant. Next, we'll look at how that arc (Chapter 4) is working for you. Finally, we'll rework your opening for maximum impact (Chapter 3).

So why go over all this again? Why not just flip back to the beginning chapters? Because they were aimed at you as the writer. Now we're talking to you as the editor. You're not in the same place where you began, even if only a few minutes have passed.

Take Time

Give yourself time between drafts. I know in real life you don't always have a lot of wiggle room. Obviously, if you're crunching out emails, you've got to move quickly. But any gap between your first write and the final go will help. Ideally, the more important the piece, the bigger the break. This pause should be included in your overall estimate for how long a writing job will take.

I've had many students tell me they need to procrastinate so panic would finally force them to write. They believed their writing has more urgency and that they could turn it out faster. Maybe that works for some people. But there's a better way: write your first draft and *then* procrastinate. You'll solve problems more easily.

In my experience, if you've actually engaged with the writing the first time around, then your mind will keep working on it after you stop, often without your noticing. The only clue may be odd-lot thoughts—*What if I flipped those two paragraphs?*—while you're taking a walk or eating a sandwich.

To capture new ideas as they roll by, I carry a tiny notebook. A phone works too. That way, when the right idea, word, or sentence pops into your head, you quickly capture it.

So, whether it's fifteen minutes, lunch time, or a couple of days, create enough breathing space to see things another way—with an editor's eyes. It's far less effort than relying on panic.

Getting Prepared for a Big-Picture Edit

For a big-picture edit, I like to print out a copy of the first draft so I can scribble corrections directly onto the page. If you're more comfortable working on a screen, add your notes there. Either way, I recommend you go through all four big-sweep steps outlined below before you begin any kind of rewrite.

When you're finished with the notations, I expect your paper (or screen) to have plenty of marks. When I taught in the University of Oregon's journalism school, students would be dismayed when handed back a marked-up paper. Even though I never graded first drafts, all those changes looked daunting. But I told them to think about the notes like a map. It would be a pretty lousy way to find treasure if your map only had three marks on it. Instead, use your first editing thoughts as a guide. You'll find your way to the end—treasure or not—if you give yourself more indications of how to get there.

Let's dive into the four steps to a big-picture edit.

1. Up the WIIFM

WIIFM is short for **W**hat's **I**n **I**t **F**or **M**e?—the most basic question all readers want you to answer. Revisit the idea of WIIFM in Chapter 1, and give your piece a high, medium, or low WIIFM rank.

Words to the Wise: Five Virtues Good Editors Share

To get yourself into an editing headspace, you need to know what makes a good editor. The best ones I've worked with all have these key mind-sets:

1. Dispassion

Editors need long (metaphorical) arms because they hold the writing in the long view. As writers, I hope we feel a certain heat about what we are trying to say. As editors, we need to be cool in our appraisals.

2. Kindness

When you function as your own editor, you'll get better results by not dissing the material. Put yourself in the helping mode—how can this be made better? It's not about bad writing. It's about good editing.

3. Firmness

On the other hand, it's okay to be demanding of the material. If the idea hasn't made it into the world in the first draft, don't despair. Focus on figuring out where the holes are and how to fill them in.

4. Delight

Editing is a game. It's a puzzle. A mystery. The writing presents problems. You find them, and then you come up with one of many ways to solve them. You get better the more you do it.

5. Finality

Editors need to let go. Writing will never be perfect. Nowhere near. But at some point, it's good enough. When you come to the end of your ability to improve it, give yourself permission to stop. There's always next time.

This is one easy way to see whether what you intended to write and what came out are the same.

For example, let's say you were writing about the history of weather trends in a certain part of the country. The goal is to let gardeners know what plants to grow. However, you get so involved with the amazing weather patterns—*Ninety consecutive days over ninety degrees*—that you don't get to the point of telling the gardeners what plants would be good. That's a seriously low (but correctable) WIIFM.

If you end up with a low WIIFM, there are a couple of options to shake things up. Sometimes it helps to talk about it with another person. They don't have to offer advice; they just have to listen to you describe what you're writing about. They can also help by writing down the words you say (see more on this technique in Chapter 12). Or you could record it on your phone. A quick free-write—focusing on the question "How will my idea solve the reader's problem?"—may also get you back on track.

2. Mind the Cable-Car Gap

Creating a cable-car sentence when you start to write can be helpful. But riding that cable car again at this point in your travels (or travails) is key to sharp editing. As part of your big-picture edit, revisit your cable-car sentence to see if your initial ideas match up with your writing.

If you didn't create a cable-car sentence when you first wrote—I know many of you plungers need to get your thoughts down before you know what you're writing about—now is the perfect time to create one (check out Chapter 3 for more details on how to do this):

In my _____ (writing category) about _____ (subject) I am saying that _____ (slant).

Check the Category

Your category is usually straightforward—either you're writing a memo, or you're not. But during the editing process, it can be helpful to do a quick gut-check on whether the structure and tone you've chosen are appropriate for your writing category.

Examine the Subject

Check to see that the subject you started with is still what you're actually writing about in your draft. Most times it is, but not always.

For instance, maybe you meant to write about a change in your company's delivery schedule. But now you discover you've written about *why* the timetable was shifted, rather than the schedule itself. By going back to the original cable-car concept, you can notice the difference between your intention and what you actually wrote.

Examine the Slant

Now that an actual draft exists, look again at your slant. Notice whether the point of your writing is the same as your draft. Sometimes your writing and your cable-car sentence are not in sync.

For example, you might be putting together a directive with a slant about why employees should follow a certain set of protocols.

In my *directive* about *the new protocols*, I am saying that *there are three important reasons why we must adopt them.*

But after you write, you realize that your slant has gone sideways. You've written about *how* to follow the protocols. You've even put in a series of steps, with only one mention of *why*. Intention and execution haven't lined up. But the cable-car sentence has done its job because you can now see the disparity.

Align Your Slant With Your Draft

If you find a gap between your cable-car sentence and what you actually wrote, you have a choice: change your writing or change your cable-car sentence.

In your directive, you can go back and rewrite the copy so it matches your original slant. In that case, you'd add the other two *why* reasons that got away.

The other possibility is to rework the cable-car sentence. It's like getting off the northbound Powell Street cable car in San Francisco and stepping onto the eastbound one traversing California Street. Both will move you along. But the new one goes in a different direction.

In this case, you might realize that the how-to is more useful to encourage employee compliance. So you'd change your slant:

In my *directive* about *the new protocols*, I am saying that *you can adopt these by following five easy steps.*

A third option would be to modify the slant so that it includes both *why* and *how* and then rewrite the piece to strengthen the *why*.

In my *directive* about *the new protocols*, I am saying that *there are three important reasons why we should adopt these and five easy steps to get there.*

Here's one more example of how the slant can shift the focus: Let's say you work for a company that makes playground equipment. You're assigned to write an article for a county's regional booster magazine about how neighbors got together and restored an aging playground—and of course they used your company's products.

Your original cable-car sentence might read:

In my *profile* about *a neighborhood playground restoration*, I am saying that *friendship between Alisha Williams and Tanya Sanchez led to benefits for the whole neighborhood.*

However, when you read through your first draft, you discover that the decision to use your company's equipment is much more prominent than the friendship of the two women.

To make it line up with the cable-car sentence, you could emphasize the friendship of the two women in the second draft.

Or you could rewrite the cable-car sentence to align with your first draft. In that case, the decision to go with your company's equipment would become the focus:

In my *profile* about *a neighborhood playground restoration*, I am saying that *the great choices of superior playground equipment led to benefits for the whole neighborhood.*

Alternatively, you could meld the two premises by changing your cable-car sentence to include both ideas:

In my *profile* about *a playground restoration*, I am saying that *friends Alisha Williams and Tanya Sanchez became savvy shoppers in their playground restoration with benefits for the whole neighborhood.*

Every time you adjust your cable-car sentence, it changes what information will be loaded on or off your cable car. If parts of the writing no longer support the new slant, they're not on board. Once you've removed anything that distracts from your overarching idea, everything left will drive you to your point and pay off.

The cable-car sentence can also show you what's missing. If you tend to write short, now's the time to look for the big holes and note where you need to write more.

3. Climb the Arc—Again

Now that you have a draft, the big-picture edit gives you a chance to examine your structure.

If you plotted an arc before you wrote, check it against what you've written. If you've avoided using an arc up to this point, go ahead and give it a try (Chapter 4).

If you have a "before" arc, compare it to your "after." You can immediately see if there are any differences. Which one works better? But even if you just have an "after" arc, check to see if the sequence of information looks good. Ask yourself, is the piece building? Are ideas where they should be? Can I move anything around to make it flow better or more logically?

Now's also a good time to do a gut-check on your choice of structure. Is it working? Is it possible there's a better one to use? If you're in doubt, go back to Chapter 6 to review your structure options once again. If you do decide to choose a different one, write your second draft to that.

4. Begin the Beginning—Again

Always be prepared to rewrite your beginning more than once. I promise this is actually a shortcut, not more work—rewrites on the beginning always pay off. Why? Because after a first draft, you've shifted your trajectory. Your view of the writing has changed, just by having done it.

Your copy might just need to be tweaked or shuffled. But the beginning is so important that you should be ready to mess with it more than any other part. It's your last chance to make a first impression. So, in order to punch up your beginning, let's go back to the original Two Minutes of Heavy Lifting exercise and do it again.

Words to the Wise: Sort Out Spaghetti Strands

As you compare your cable-car sentence with your initial draft, you may discover more than one major idea in your piece. I think of these additional thoughts as spaghetti strands. They're often twisted up around themselves in the writing.

Spaghetti strands can be golden. Untangle them from the surrounding writing and you'll have several bonus ideas with almost no effort. Each idea can be developed separately. Right now, you can write about the most important or most interesting strand and leave the rest for another time.

For example, let's say you're writing a piece about the benefits of a new device your company has created. In your first draft, you've included a description of the new device. You've also written a backstory about the struggle to develop the device. And you have a profile of the person who fought to make it happen. In this draft, each of these three strands keeps popping up, which makes your story complicated and unfocused. Which of these will be the main point?

In your rewrite, you'd focus on one strand, like highlighting the benefits of the device. You'd save the information about the development and the staff members for future stories.

Begin Later Than You Think

One more thing about beginnings: sometimes they start too early. You may be surprised to find that your writing bumps up a notch when you get several paragraphs in. This is common in first drafts. It's been dubbed "literary throat clearing." Writers beat around the bush before getting to the point. They want to set up the story. They feel the need to insert important details first. Look for your own "ahems."

In the rewrite, ask yourself, "What's the point where this story really takes off?" Cut everything ahead of that moment. For instance, here's a cable-car sentence for a piece I wrote a few years ago:

In my *personal essay* about *my camp counselor Dottie*, I am saying that *she pretended to be inept so that her campers would become leaders*.

However, in a first read-through of the draft, Dottie doesn't show up until halfway into the piece. If this is about her and her wily ways, she can't be introduced so late. To fix it, I added a scene featuring Dottie right at the top of the story. The stronger beginning supported the rest of the essay and helped me get rid of extra words and ideas.

Write On Exercise: Two Minutes of Heavy Lifting—Redux

Time: Three minutes

Forget anything you've written. That's good. Sit down with a timer and respond to the questions.

Step 1. What's this piece of writing about? (45 seconds)

Step 2. Why is it being told? (30 seconds)

Step 3. How does it connect to the greater world? (20 seconds)

Step 4. What's the point? (15 seconds)

Step 5. In one word, what's this about? (10 seconds)

Your one word may not be the same one you started with. That's OK. You get to decide which one you want. Whether the word is the same or not, as an editing technique, I want you to take one last step.

Step 6. What is the best illustration of that word? (45 seconds)

It could be a story, a scene, an explanation, a grabber question, a sharp observation, or a summation.

Now look at the way you actually started your first draft. Is that the best illustration of your chosen word now? For your second draft, use the answer to the question above to rewrite the beginning of your piece.

Write, Rewrite, or Tweak?

Writing is rewriting. So how much do you need to do? The answer comes from how close the writing aligns with your cable-car sentence. Sometimes, depending on length, it's easier just to create a completely new draft. Other times, you can rewrite sections by moving ideas around, changing how things move up the arc, or inserting the connecting ideas that will make it work.

But in this overview work, don't get hung up on fiddly changes. Fussing over word choices at this point is a waste of time. What if you later decide to throw the whole paragraph out? Or worse, you don't throw it out because you've worked too hard on it? Keep thinking big for this first sweep through your work.

Real-World Review: Spaghetti Strands Provide Plenty of Material

Author and linguist Rosemarie Ostler knows how to draft for quick results.

Since 2003, Rosemarie has written about the odd, fascinating, and historic aspects of American speech. As an American language expert, she frequently contributes to magazines and has written four books including *Founding Grammars: How Early America's War over Words Shaped Today's Language.* Her steady output demands an economic use of time in both drafting and editing.

She always starts with a fast first draft. "It doesn't have to be good," she says. "It just has to be down on the page." Then, she uses a big-picture edit to dig through the material and pull out spaghetti strands. "I put all the ideas out there, and then I winnow."

Here is her shaggy first draft pitch letter to a magazine editor. I've picked out and numbered the spaghetti strands.

We often hear complaints that texting and tweeting are turning young people into a bunch of emoticon-using semi-illiterates. What a surprise, then, that a recent Dictionary.com poll found that millennials were the group most concerned about grammar and usage online. Around 74 percent reported being annoyed by grammar and spelling mistakes on social media, a higher percentage than any other group. (#1 strand—story on millennials' unexpected grammar preferences)

We don't really need a survey to know that grammar issues are still very much alive. Googling "bad grammar" brings up over half a million hits. (#2 strand—story on the massive online interest in grammar) *What's more, the discussions often revolve around the same arbitrary rules that were first laid down in eighteenth-century grammar books—don't split infinitives, don't end a sentence with a preposition. The internet is perpetuating traditional grammar rules.* (#3 strand—a look at how the Internet is supporting conventional grammar prohibitions)

My article will explore the trend of online grammar advice and show the continuity from old-fashioned language study of earlier times to the issues that concern people now. (#2 strand again) *I'll take a look at popular grammar blogs such as Grammar Girl and Grammarphobia and the types of advice they give.* (#2 or #3) *I'll also discuss how the increased presence of genuine language experts—linguists and copy editors among others—may be changing the online grammar conversation.* (#4 strand—how experts' online contributions may be affecting grammar usage—perhaps for the better)

Wow—that's four ideas in three paragraphs.

Once Rosemarie locates the entwined strands, "I go through and pick out what looks like it could be a theme statement," she explains. After that, it's a matter of which one appeals to her. In this case, she chose strand #2, the massive online interest in grammar.

But those other ideas aren't forgotten. "I will go on to develop them," says Rosemary. Each may be a complete story, slanted to different magazines' needs.

That's an efficient process.

CHAPTER 9

The Medium-Focus Edit

Writing Problem: *I've done my big-picture edit, but my writing still feels weak.*

Rx: *Four fast tactics help you create clarity and power.*

In this chapter, we'll look at four editing steps to shape up any writing—no matter the length, style, or subject. If you're in a hurry, these are quick tools you can turn to after a big-picture edit.

The top fix? A handy verb checkup. If you did nothing else but examine your verb choices, your next draft would be better. After that, we'll shoebox paragraphs to make sure your thoughts are in order. And then we'll delve into the unseen logic that flows between paragraphs. Last is a look at pronouns—and why you're missing a bet if you don't re-examine them.

The **Write On Exercise: On the Word Count** will help you identify unconscious rhythms, make swift cuts, and control your pacing. **Cheat Sheet: The Ancient and Mighty Verbs** offers inspiration for finding strong verbs. In the **Real-World Review: Advice from the Editor's Desk**, Kathleen Brenzel gives you an insider's editing viewpoint.

Tackling the Medium-Focus Edit

Editing is a step-by-step process. Right now, you're in between that wide-sweep edit that checks major concepts and the final close-up that hunts down the picky details. But if you were horribly rushed for time, the suggestions in the medium-focus edit could stand alone. Even if you just follow these, your writing will be better.

If you're reading this book chronologically, you may have already written a second draft based on the big-picture edit ideas in Chapter 8. That puts you in the perfect spot to start using these four techniques.

But don't worry if you're still on your first draft. Dive in right here. By using these approaches, you may be able to solve problems that have evaded solution so far.

Also, I've put the four pillars of the medium-focus edit—verb review, shoeboxing paragraphs, unseen logic, and pronoun spotting—in my preferred order of usefulness. And if you've completely run out of time, do the Write On Exercise for the quickest possible fix.

Review Your Verbs

No matter what shape your writing is in at the moment, upgrading your verbs can help. Unlike other languages, English devotes just 30 percent of its words to verbs. That means these valuable drivers of thought need to be carefully considered in a rewrite. Strong verbs can carry a piece.

Hunt Down the Verbs

To start, go through your piece and highlight every verb. Once you've got them all selected, go back and see how many fall into the "to be" category. (See the Cheat Sheet on page 152 for all their manifestations.)

So what's wrong with *to be* verbs? In English, certain tenses need them as the helpers to the main verbs.

I *am* going.

We *have* built.

You *should have* lifted when I said so.

In many situations, we use *to be* verbs simply because that's the way we talk. When we speak, the words blow right through the minds of the listeners. When we write, the words are fixed in the material world. Therefore, they need to work harder to earn their place on the page. And verbs are often the best way to add more power.

Make a Verb Switch

See if you can substitute stronger verbs for the casual *is* or *was*. For instance, consider this motorbike sentence:

The street *was* crowded with blaring motorbikes.

You could give a stronger picture of the street by removing *was* and turning *crowded* from an adjective to a verb:

Blaring motorbikes *crowded* the street.

Try this example:

My birthday *is* next week.

A verb change could send an emotional signal rather than just a fact. The verb works harder to convey your feelings:

My birthday *looms* next week.

When you're hunting down *to be* verbs, you'll often find them accompanied by the words *there* or *it*. Nothing is inherently wrong with either of those words. In fact, in the Telegraph of London's online post, "30 Great Openings in Literature," seven of the contenders begin with *it* (Including my favorite—Jane Austen's *Pride and Prejudice*: "It is a truth to be universally acknowledged, that a single man in possession of a good fortune, must be in want of a wife.")

However, as a reluctant writer, your literary ambitions might not aim that high. So I suggest you use *there* and *it* as red flags. They will lead you to discover which verbs you might want to beef up.

For example, in this sentence you could get more definitive with your verb choice.

There *were* five rows of kale in the field.

Cut *there were*. Make *five rows* the subject. Then add a more descriptive verb, based on what you actually saw:

Five rows of kale *marched* or *straggled* or *danced* or *wilted* across the field.

The last red flag for changing *to be* verbs is the word *that*. Often the verb in the phrase following *that* can be moved to the front of the sentence.

It *is* the river that weaves through the fjords.

Weaves is a great verb. So drop *it is*. Get rid of *that*.

The river *weaves* through the fjords.

Check the Rest

Examine other verbs. Are they working as hard as they could?

To find out, check adverbs. They're your red flags. These words—that end in *ly* and describe verbs—let you know when a verb is weak. When you spot them, make a change. For example, instead of *He spoke rudely*, you could write *He interrupted*. Or, you could rephrase *They walked slowly*, to *They meandered*. You don't need the adverb to get the point across.

Sometimes adverbs hide what actually happened. For clarity, you might want to recast the sentence *The meeting ended badly*, to *The participants shouted at each other when they left the room*.

One caution with verb swaps: you don't want fancy words if you don't need them. Always consider the tone and context of your writing. And try not to let your thesaurus show. In the Dr. Oz newspaper column, no one ever *eats*. Instead, they always *munch*, *chew*, *crunch*, or *chow down*. I know the goal is to create interest—but please, couldn't we occasionally just *eat* a vegetable?

On the other hand, the world is full of so many dynamic verbs (see Cheat Sheet: The Ancient and the Mighty for a few of my favorites). Why not try some on for size?

Get Tense

Finally, while you peruse your verbs, check your tense. Is it the same throughout? Notice if you are shifting between tenses without a reason. Decide which you need and stick to it.

Most writing stays in one tense—either past, present, or future. However, you can deliberately mix your tenses. When working with stories or themes that intertwine, hopping back and forth between past and present tense can signal the reader about a shift in time or place. Working in present tense gives your writing an immediacy. But it's a trade-off. In the present, you lose the ability to look back and make sense of what has happened.

Whatever you decide, follow a consistent pattern.

Shoebox Your Paragraphs

Shoeboxing is an editing technique that allows you to identify the thoughts within each paragraph. This labeling also gives you clues about where you repeat the same ideas. Spend a moment labeling and you'll bring order to your writing. Here's how it's done.

Name That Paragraph

Go through your copy. On the margin, beside each paragraph, ask yourself, if this particular paragraph were stuffed in a shoebox, what would the label on the outside say? These labels should only be a few words long. Shoeboxing helps you discover several common writing problems.

- **Two subjects:** For clarity, a paragraph should only be about one thing. Any time you find yourself making a label with the word *and*, you have two different ideas. The easy fix is to break apart the information into two paragraphs. And yes, unless you're turning out formal or academic writing, a single sentence can comprise a paragraph.
- **Same subjects:** Each label should be different. Occasionally, you might find yourself wanting to put the same label on paragraphs separated by other writing in between. Move the paragraphs around until they are near each other and see where the overlap in thought occurs. One paragraph may say it better. Or you might be able to consolidate the information into a single paragraph. Or reshape one so it says something different.
- **Too wordy:** Sometimes you'll find it hard to sum up what's in your paragraph. If this happens, ask yourself follow-up questions: *What's the point of this paragraph?* Or *what would happen if I chucked this paragraph out?* If the answer is "nothing," go ahead and cut it on the spot. But usually, you'll discover why it's necessary. Then you can narrow your word choice for the label and rewrite the paragraph to fit.

Cheat Sheet: The Ancient and the Mighty

Check your use of *to be* and substitute stronger verbs where you can.

To Be Verb

is	could	would	had
am	shall	do	may
are	should	does	might
was	be	did	must
were	been	has	
can	will	have	

Powerful/Fun/Useful Verbs

These are a few of my favorite verbs. Let them inspire your own choices.

abandon	deceive	obfuscate
abdicate	deign	offend
accentuate	demur	pervade
admonish	disparage	precede
advise	doubt	press
afford	dream	quash
alleviate	elucidate	recant
announce	emote	recapitulate
arise	epitomize	refuse
articulate	extol	repair
assuage	forge	rescue
bifurcate	greet	skip
blot	hammer	spoil
brake	hector	stultify
burst	implore	subjugate
capitulate	ingratiate	tout
circumvent	interrupt	transform
collect	juxtapose	vacillate
comprise	launch	vie
construe	match	wane
coruscate	maximize	winnow
damage	mollify	yield

Look at the Patterns

With shoeboxing, you can check to see if your ideas are flowing from one point to the next. By examining each label, you can see whether the story builds or the information is sequenced in the way you want. You can even set up your labels as steps up the arc. (For arc structure, see Chapter 4.)

If you're telling a complicated story—perhaps one that braids together several storylines—shoeboxing also shows you the points where the themes cross and allows you to easily rearrange the paragraphs.

For instance, let's say your company sells flour products. You're writing about the rise (so to speak) of a successful artisanal bakery that uses those products. The shoebox labels for a rough first draft might go like this:

- Introduction to the bakery
- Owner's first experience baking
- Family history in baking
- Sourcing the trees for the wood-fired ovens
- Search for other artisanal bread recipes
- Acquiring the wood-fired ovens
- Why no yeast breads—slow rise only
- Winning prizes
- Owner's reaction to success
- Owner's children carry it forward

When you look at your labels, you realize you have several threads of story here. You have the chronology of the business—its climb to success from humble beginnings. But you also have a thread about the mechanics—the ovens, the wood, no yeast breads, and so on. And you have the owner's family story: Who supported him? What drove his vision?

This is a lot of material. But once you see the three threads, you can divide them into chunks of thought. You could rearrange the labels—and therefore the paragraphs—in many ways. Here's one possibility.

Start with the success. It hooks the reader in. Back up into the history, twining the personal and bakery's advancement together and jumping away to explain the mechanics when the reader needs that background information. The second draft might look like this:

- Introduction to the bakery
- Winning prizes
- Owner's reaction to success

(transition)

- Family history in baking
- Owner's first experience baking as a boy

(transition)

- Why no yeast breads?
- Acquiring the wood-fired ovens
- Sourcing the trees for the wood-fired ovens

(transition)

- Search for other artisanal bread recipes
- Owner's children carry it forward

Now, when you polish it, you can pay special attention to those transitions to make sure readers smoothly jump from one section to the next.

Check the Unseen Connections

In Terry Pratchett's Discworld fantasy books, the Unseen University is the magicians' seat of learning. It's the source of disastrous magical spells that interfere with the lives of ordinary people. I think of the unseen connections in writing the same way. Not that most reluctant writers have to deal with magical explosions or a cranky orangutan for a librarian. But if the unwritten logic that connects paragraphs or even whole sections isn't examined, it can derail your writing without your ever knowing why.

What do I mean by unseen connections? Basically, each paragraph of your writing is linked. You had a reason to write one and then the next. When you check for the unwritten logic, you're looking for the thought or idea that ties one paragraph to the next. Sometimes it's obvious. That's great. Other times, you can't find the link. Perhaps the connecting idea hasn't made it into your writing yet. By trying to name it, you'll discover the words you need to make the transition happen. A quick round of defining the unseen connections can give you confidence that your writing is shaping up the way you want it to go.

Write the Unwritten

Between each paragraph, add a phrase or sentence that describes what ties the two together. You can write it as a question that readers might ask at the end of the paragraph that would launch your writing into the next idea: "Why would I want to know about rubber grommets?"

Here's an example of unseen connections written out for several paragraphs for a lifestyle advice blog about bringing your "real self" to work:

Recent studies have pointed to the idea that people are their least authentic selves at work. That means many of us are spending forty hours a week (or sometimes a lot more) wearing a mask. And this phony behavior can become a source of deep unhappiness in our lives.

Unwritten question: "Really? Do I need this advice?"

If you find yourself fuming on the ride home about work concerns, or snapping at some hapless person who bumped into you on the street, you may want to take your job-related stress down a notch.

Unwritten question: "How can I do that?"

The bad news is that donning a mask to go to work is a habit— and we all know habits are hard to break. The good news is that you can retrain yourself. Consider it a journey, with small, but thoughtful steps. That can add up to real change in your happiness levels.

Unwritten question: "What do I have to do?"

This game plan will allow you to keep it real—even at work.

Edit With the Unseen

As an editing tool, unseen connections help in several ways. On the most basic level, they can show you if your thoughts are out of order or could be arranged more strategically. Here are a few problems that will show up using unseen connections:

- **Missing material:** If you can't name the connection, that's a good clue material is missing. Go back and fill in anything you need to make your paragraphs move smoothly. That way, readers won't suffer whiplash by being snapped from one thought to the next.
- **Mismatched ideas:** Sometimes, the unseen question and the following paragraph don't match. If so, go through your draft, hunt down a paragraph that satisfies the question, and move it into place. Or fill in with a new paragraph that will answer the reader's need at that point.
- **Overwritten transitions:** The last sentence in one paragraph and the first in the next need to form some relationship, but they shouldn't repeat the same information. Tightening those wordy sentences will sharpen the transition. Working with the unseen also makes it easier to create those sentences that lead off and close paragraphs. (See Chapter 10 for more ideas on creating tight transitions.)
- **Too many words:** Taking care of the unseen connections helps with wordiness. If you've been able to sum up the connection in a word, a phrase, or a question, how many more words do you need in the actual writing? Could you cut?

Pick Your Pronouns

The last medium-focus edit technique involves a quick pass to find more descriptive substitutes for your pronouns. Of course we all write with *he*, *she*, *they*, *them*, *we*, *it*, and *you*. It's the way we think. However, with this edit, we'll use them as red flags: your writing might get more exact if you replaced a pronoun with a suitable detail. Most pronouns will stay. But check on them. You'll become aware of the few spots where your writing could be stronger by swapping pronouns out for more specifics.

Search for the Pronouns

Go through and circle or highlight every pronoun you can find. After you find them, think about substitutions. Sometimes, instead of *he* or *it*, you can find other descriptors that will enlarge a reader's understanding and strengthen the writing.

For example, let's say you're reporting on a scientific study of organic versus conventional dairy products. Here's the sentence:

It concludes that the dairy products of cows fed on organic grass show no discernible health benefits for the public.

The *it* is the name of the study you've already mentioned. But you could tuck in valuable reader information by removing *it* and adding a description:

The report, funded by the Dairyman's Herbicide Association, concludes that the dairy products of cows fed on organic grass show no discernible health benefits for the public.

Here's another one. You've interviewed a popular bartender in a local establishment. You've named him. And then you write:

He stood behind the bar, flipping bottles, and serving cocktails.

After circling your pronoun, try switching it out for a more exact description:

In command of the bar, his hands flashed, flipping bottles and serving cocktails.

Do you see him better now?

The Benefits of the Medium-Focus Edit

Many reluctant writers find these four editing steps—plus the Write On Exercise—to be the most helpful in the book. Swapping out verbs and pronouns is a quick way to power up your writing. Labeling the paragraphs and naming the connections between them will go a long way toward clear, logical thought. Follow these four and you're well on your way to improving *how* you write in whatever you *have* to write.

Write On Exercise:
On the Word Count

Time: Depends on length of writing

This fast—and painless—exercise puts you in charge of sentence size. It's as easy as counting. I first learned the process from a thirty-year writing veteran and consultant, Barbara Winslow Boardman.

Step 1. Go Down for the Count Take a paragraph—or three—of your writing. It doesn't matter where you start. Go through and above each sentence, write in the number of words it contains. Do that for several paragraphs. Then write the numbers out in a line. A paragraph might look like this—24, 20, 18, 21, 26, 31. Another one could look like this—5, 17, 11, 5, 26, 9.

Step 2. Check Your Patterns Which of these paragraphs would lull you to sleep? Which would wake you up? We tend to write in a pattern. From the moment we hear our mother's heartbeat, we are all creatures of rhythm. We write to our own inner beats. This little exercise shows you what they are. You can use it to your advantage.

Step 3. Change It Up For readers' interest, vary the pace of your sentences. If most are the same length, try cutting up a few. If all of them are short and choppy, consider how to extend or combine them.

Real-World Review: Advice from an Editor's Desk

Kathleen Brenzel shares the most common mistakes writers make.

When it comes to editing, Kathleen Brenzel has seen it all. During her long and distinguished career as an editor at *Sunset, the Magazine of Western Living*, she oversaw four editions of the encyclopedic *Sunset Western Garden Book*, as well as countless other projects. I can't imagine how many articles have crossed Kathleen's desk. She's an all-round editing rock star.

I had the pleasure of working with her on a book in 2006. Her editing skills always enhanced my words. So I asked her, what are the most common writing mistakes she's seen?

Here are her top picks.

Backing Into a Story

"I have a problem when writers ramble on before they get to the point," Kathleen says. "If they don't draw me in, I won't read any more." This is true, she says, for the opening of a letter, or any kind of text. The editing fix? Get to the point quickly or set a compelling scene in the first paragraph that, as Kathleen says, "puts the reader right into what you're telling them about."

Weak Verbs

"Use active verbs more than anything else," Kathleen advises. "They give immediacy to whatever you're doing. They get people into the action." Kathleen cites a recent *Sunset* article by writer Susan Casey on experiencing the sunrise at the peak of Hawaii's Haleakalā. "Look at those verbs— the altitude *rises*, they *witness*, the procession of cars *winds*, mountain peaks *tower*—active, active, active."

Readers Left with Unanswered Questions

"Never open a door you cannot close," said Walter Doty, *Sunset's* editor-in-chief from 1939 to 1954. "His advice came down to me," Kathleen explains, "through the annals of *Sunset*." It means that writers shouldn't raise an issue that brings up unanswered questions. "You have to anticipate," she says. "You don't want readers hanging with a question. If you don't deal with the details, they'll say, 'Wait a minute, you're not telling me the whole story.'" Sometimes adding an extra sentence of explanation does the job.

Lack of Clarity

This happens when part of a writer's idea hasn't made it to the page. "Readers form a picture in their minds of the situation," Kathleen says. "But they're not inside the writer's head. They don't know what you're thinking. You need to help them by providing all the necessary information."

The Same Idea in More Than One Place

It happens. "In the frenzy of writing that first draft, you put in things out of order," Kathleen observes. "You say the same thing with different words in different places." Her suggestion: "Go back over what you've done. Reread and reread again. You'll always find something."

Careless Mistakes

"Nothing turns an editor off more than lazy mistakes," Kathleen says. "It makes them question the writer's abilities." These include:

- Not researching your editor's areas of responsibility— Kathleen says, "Don't send food recipes to the garden editor."
- Not researching your target publication's history—"Has it been done a zillion times recently?"
- Ignoring small goofs—"Using present and past tense in the same sentence."

On the other hand, says Kathleen, a well-aimed, appropriate communication reflects positively on the writer. She appreciates "polished text that the writer has taken the time to look over before sending it to me." Whether it's an email pitch letter or a response to a potential client, Kathleen says, "Put your best foot forward. Write clearly. Write carefully. Target your pitch. And know your field."

CHAPTER 10

Pointer Sentences Put You in Charge

Writing Problem: *My writing jumps from thought to thought.*

Rx: *Add pointer sentences to guide your reader.*

Readers want clarity. You can pack your writing with great information, but if you jump from idea to idea without clear transitions, your readers will quickly give up. The fix? Add powerful controlling sentences at the beginning and end of paragraphs. I call these *pointer sentences* because they point readers in the direction you want them to go.

For this next editing step, we'll look at how to strengthen your writing with punchy pointer sentences. This chapter also includes **Write On Exercise: Scan for Fun and Profit** to examine pointers for clarity and communication. You can also check out 12 ways to move material in **Cheat Sheet: Transitions Checklist**. The **Real-World Review: Burying the Lead** demonstrates how I dug up the most interesting idea and placed it where it needed to go—right up front with a pointer sentence.

Now's the Time for Pointers

Writers are often encouraged to construct pointer sentences when they start their writing process—either in the first draft or even before that in a formal outline. However, many reluctant writers hate dealing with these sentences then, because they don't know where their writing is headed. Or even if they have a general sense, until it gets into a draft, it's in a state of flux. When you're still corralling your thoughts, trying to formulate a specific sentence to nowhere is damned difficult and painful; it's an experience in failure.

So while it might seem counter-intuitive, I recommend constructing pointer sentences when you edit, rather than when you first write. By focusing on pointers after you've got a draft complete, you're in a much better place to shape the writing and drive your points home. Even if you've already written pointer sentences, go back and sharpen them when you edit. You'll gain more control over your material and fast-track your finished product.

Signposts Lead the Way

Pointer sentences that start a paragraph usually have names like *topic* or *focus*. At the beginning of newspaper articles they're called *lead* or *lede* sentences (pronounced *leed*). However, I like to call the starting pointers *signpost sentences* because I can visualize the old-fashioned roadside signposts shaped like arrows—*Jamesport: 2 miles*. Signpost sentences show the way. They let the reader know what to expect.

To start working with signposts, go through your draft starting with the second paragraph—save the first for last—and look at the first sentences for each paragraph. Ask yourself, *Do I have a clear sentence that points the reader in the right direction? Is the sentence working hard enough? Are there any extra words I could cut? Is there another, better way to direct the reader?*

Sometimes you'll discover that the signpost sentence—*look this way*—hasn't arrived yet. If that's the case, do a short form of shoeboxing (Chapter 9). Ask yourself, *If the contents of this paragraph were sitting in a shoebox on a shelf, what would the label say?* From that label, construct your signpost sentence.

Finally, go back and examine your signpost sentence in the very first paragraph. I've mentioned before that paying close attention to the beginning pays off. This pointer sentence is the granddaddy of them all. Depending on your editing process, you might have rewritten your beginning once or twice. Now check it again. Is this the best illustration of your point? Would any adjustments make it better? Does it set up reader curiosity? Or is a thought still missing? Now's the time to add it.

Signposts in Action

Signposts have a lot of jobs to do. Here's a few examples of how they can work and what happens when they're missing.

For instance, in this programmer's email, the signpost highlights the main directive:

> **As discussed in the meeting, the current recommendation is to hold off using the E2015 syntax in runtime Shakti files.** *We need a complete analysis on the associated transpiled payload and computational increases. At this time, it appears transpilation adds a 30–800 percent increase. Further analysis will be done in Q1 or Q2 to find a path forward. Some language features can be used without worry and are listed in the memo. If you have any questions, please feel free to comment on the memo or drop by for a chat.*

In this personal essay, the signpost sentence functions as a change in perspective. It adds a grownup point of view to the child's experience.

> **When I was four years old, I had no concept that the house we lived in was actually a safe place to ride out floods.** *The night the river rose, I hung onto the back pockets of my two older brothers' jeans when they grappled with the kitchen door leading to the basement. I crowded in small between them. We peered into the darkness. Bob's flashlight beam rippled over the swirling water. The cellar steps were getting sucked into the black swamp. What would happen when they all disappeared?*

Here's an example without a signpost sentence. You have to arrive at the end before you find out what these people are doing. And you still don't know where they are.

> *At sunset we left our shoes in the sand and waded into the calm sea. We shuffled along in the shallow water. The hard-packed surface underfoot betrayed nothing. Maria gave a shout. With balletic grace, her body tall and straight, she extended her leg up out of the water. There, clutched in her perfectly curled toes, was the largest clam I'd ever seen.*

Notice the first sentence doesn't cover what's in the paragraph. It's not serving as a signpost. Why keep the readers in the dark? Why not say the group is in Baja, hunting for clams with their feet? For clarity, you could start with:

> *A fresh clam dinner from the Sea of Cortez was right under our feet.*

Or, if you don't want to give it all away:

> *Clamming in Baja did not involve fancy equipment.*

The Springboard Sentence

As strong as they are, signpost sentences don't work alone. They have a quiet partner. When making a transition of thought, a lot depends on how the previous paragraph ended. I think of these final sentences as *springboards*. In gymnastics, the springboard allows a gymnast to launch into the air. In writing, springboard sentences seamlessly boost readers into the next paragraph.

Here's an example of a springboard and pointer working together. In this profile about a vegetarian restaurant owner, one paragraph ends with:

> *Long before the movie came out, he named his first restaurant Ratatouille.* **That's because, Raymond says, "Those ingredients say 'vegetarian.'"**

And the beginning of the next:

> **Now, Ratatouille also says, "Fast, healthy food on-the-go."** *Raymond serves vegetarian breakfast, lunch, and dinner in recycled cardboard boxes. Take-away meals outnumber sit-downs four to one.*

Just as the shoeboxing exercise helps create signposts, the unseen logic exercise (Chapter 9 again) assists you with springboards. Name the unseen connection between the end of one paragraph and the start of the next. Then you'll see if you need a springboard sentence or if it's working hard enough.

Go through your own writing and look at the unwritten logic that ties one paragraph to the next. Check your springboards. Is the thought transition abrupt? Are pointers missing? Is there a way to tighten them?

Write On Exercise: Scan for Fun and Profit

Time: Depends on length of writing

The challenge in this exercise: can you communicate with only signposts and springboards?

Step 1. Copy and paste. Put each of your signposts and springboards onto a blank page. You can also print out your piece and mark with a highlighter if that's your style.

Step 2. Read all pointers aloud. If you have a writing buddy, read to them.

Step 3. Ask yourself, *Is the information or story clear?* If you're using an arc, does the information build? Can you spot any holes?

Step 4. Add and polish. Based on what you find, go back and fix.

Step. 5. Cut elsewhere. Now that those sentences are working harder, look for cuts you could make in the rest of the writing for cleaner copy.

Transitions—Will Work for Change

Signposts and springboards are the directive devices. **How** we actually move is the transition. Transitions in life are not easy. We have the biggies—birth, death, graduation, first job, promotion, moving, divorce, first child, first book. Transitions are the thresholds we step over into another space. We rarely go back. Just changing your mind about something is a transition. It takes time, energy, and often strong emotion to do a 180.

In writing, solid transitions allow readers to move from one thought to the next without whiplash, or resistance, or even too much awareness that they're being pulled along. You want them to follow your thought.

Transitions function as the set-up for your next piece of information. In a narrative, they allow you to ground the reader in time and space.

It's a challenge to create good steering ideas. Because transitions are hard, we tend to use the same ones over and over. Here are 12 to try. It's not a definitive list, but focus on these and you'll power up your writing.

1. Transition of Opposites

Opposites can be used as a hook. Think of the classic opening of Dickens' *Great Expectations*: "It was the best of times, it was the worst of times..." When you set up arguments, opinion pieces, or persuasive writing, you depend on reverse transitions. They allow you to go against a reader's expectations. Transitions of opposites use signal words like *however, on the other hand, but*—and yes, except for more formal or academic writing, *but* can start a sentence.

> **Example:** *Many people think lenticular cloud formations presage a significant weather event. However, they don't.* You would then start your next paragraph with the reason the clouds don't signal a change.

2. Transition of Time

This transition tells readers how much time has elapsed. Time can also shift back and forth with signal words like *back then, now, meanwhile, yesterday, in the afternoon, tomorrow, last month,* or *last year*.

Example: *On Thursday, August 9, 1956, the march to Pretoria began as women gathered at the Union Buildings.*

3. Transition of Place

Locating the action can be as simple as *at the top of the building.* Or, that old classic, *Meanwhile, back on the ranch.* Moving readers from one place to another requires a pointer sentence that describes the shift. The signal words for transitions of place are those that begin phrases like—*at, by, down, in, on, up,* etc.

Example: *In the offices of Ha and McGruder....*

4. Transition as Jump Cut

We know about jump cuts from movies. Time collapses between one scene and the next. Two characters smile at each other. Jump cut to both lying in a rumpled bed.

In writing, jump cuts play with both time and space. They're especially useful if you're braiding two stories together. For instance, let's say you're writing about saving an historic building. You might jump cut between how the protesters are organizing, and how the heavy equipment operators are preparing for demolition. Readers know that at some point, these two sides will meet. Jump cuts rely on the same signal words you use for transitions of time and place, but now the action is faster.

Example: *Leo brags, "My car will never be towed."*

(Jump cut)

On the quiet street, a red Lamborghini slowly winches up the tow truck's ramp.

5. Transition with Quotes

Quotes can be a swift way to reveal the nature of the speaker or move the action along. That's why they're often used in profiles. Ask yourself where you want the piece to go next and then see if you have a quote that covers it. A caution: don't use quotes for simple facts, even if the speaker says them. You can sum those up. Quotes should add color, authenticity, and support to your slant. They leave a memorable impression.

Example: *"No matter how early in the morning the exhibits arrive,"* Kim Phan says, *"I have to be there when the displays come into the building."* The piece could then continue with more stories about the museum director's dedication.

6. Transition as Question

Question transitions are straightforward. They ask the question the reader should be thinking about at this point. *So where's all this going?* And then you answer that. Use questions with restraint. More than one or two can feel condescending to the reader.

Example: In a blog post for a jobs website, you describe the cement footing of a highway bridge being scaled by roped-in climbers. You ask *Want to join them on the ropes as a bridge safety inspector?* What would follow was how readers could do that.

7. Transition with Facts

You can use interesting or unusual facts to create transitions. I've heard author and writing coach Don Fry refer to certain facts as "gold coins," dropped into the material for readers to pick up. However, gold coins can't be arbitrary or off-track. They need to enlarge the readers' understanding or enjoyment of the information.

Example: In a blog post for an old-car website, the springboard sentence goes—*Under the hood of Volvo's 122 series were modified tractor engines.* That factoid leads to the start of the next paragraph—*Those Swedish workhorses were simple for any weekend car tinkerer to figure out.* And after that, you could describe the various maintenance tasks.

8. Transition of Point of View

Changing from one person's viewpoint to another is similar to a transition of opposites. However, here the changes rely on putting yourself in various people's shoes. For example, you could round up different opinions on a subject and then shift from one person's take to another. Sometimes the shift is from someone you're describing to your own point of view. Signal phrases like *however*, *but*, and *on the other hand* let readers know. It could be as simple as *The crowd disagrees.*

Example: You might end one paragraph with—*Mr. Marcellinus is cautious.* Start the next with—*Despite the setbacks, Ms. Shaw remains enthusiastic.* And go on to say why she feels that way.

9. Transition as One-Liner

This one is simple. You're heading in one direction and then—with a sentence or even a single word—you turn around and go another way. These often consist of a one-sentence paragraph. Signal words are short and sharp like *not so much, forget it, right,* and *okay.*

Example: *I saw myself coming home. I would be gracious. Everyone would hug.*

Not.

No one showed up.

10. Transition as Observation

Here's where you get to comment on the action. Writers are often hesitant to editorialize, but your opinion can be a quick shortcut through the facts.

Example: You have to describe what the company's new warehouse looks like. You'd end one paragraph with the facts—*A series of twenty-foot-tall shelves holds the storage boxes.* Make the transition with your observation—*That's a lot of shelving.* Then go on with details of how people cope with the massive system.

11. Transition as Compaction

This is where you take the action of a paragraph or a section and squash it into a couple of sentences. You put your spin on it. This compaction is commonly used in sports writing, where the previous paragraphs describe the details of the plays and end with the writer's quick observation. To find compactions, start this sentence in your head—*in other words...*—and then fill in the blanks.

Example: A basketball game has been described. Now comes the compaction. *The game ran into four tied overtimes.* That sets up the scenelet at the end. *In the stands, even those putting on their coats stood still.*

12. Transition as Summation

Rather than compacting action, as in the previous transition, here you sum up ideas that have been driving the writing. These can occur at the beginning or ending of a section or piece. Signal words might be *in addition, therefore, it follows that, now, consequently,* or *as a result.* Try to avoid clichés like *at the end of the day.* It's interesting to me that in informal writing, the word *so* acts like the word *hark* did in ancient times. It means, *Listen up. I'm going to tell you something important.*

Example: *So, for all these years the speaker has remained steadfast in his opinions. But now society has shifted its views.*

Cheat Sheet: Quick Check for Transitions

1. Transition of Opposites
Many people think lenticular cloud formations presage a significant weather event. However, they don't.

2. Transition of Time
On Thursday, August 9, 1956, the march to Pretoria began as women gathered at the Union Buildings.

3. Transition of Place
In the offices of Ha and McGruder...

4. Transition as Jump Cut
Leo brags, "My car will never be towed." (Jump cut) On the quiet street, the red Lamborghini slowly winches up the tow truck's ramp.

5. Transition with Quotes

"No matter how early in the morning the exhibits arrive," Kim Phan says, "I have to be there when the displays come into the building."

6. Transition as Question

Want to join them on the ropes as a bridge safety inspector?

7. Transition with Facts

Under the hood of Volvo's 122 series were modified tractor engines.

Those Swedish workhorses were simple for any weekend car tinkerer to figure out.

8. Transition of Point of View

Mr. Marcellinus is cautious.

Despite the setbacks, Ms. Shaw remains enthusiastic.

9. Transition as One-Liner

I saw myself coming home. I would be gracious. Everyone would hug.

Not.

No one showed up.

10. Transition as Observation

A series of twenty-foot-tall shelves holds the storage boxes. That's a lot of shelving.

11. Transition as Compaction

The game ran into four tied overtimes. In the stands, even those putting on their coats stood still.

12. Transition as Summation

So, for all these years the speaker has remained steadfast in his opinions. But now society has shifted its views.

Dare to Direct

At this level of editing, you take charge of your material. Don't hesitate to be directive. Readers hate to be left in the dark. They prefer writers who firmly tell them where to look—even if they disagree with what they're looking at. If you arrive at this end of your writing, and you feel your voice is too strong, you can always go back and add qualifiers.

But I'll bet money you won't.

Real-World Review: Burying the Lead

The language of journalism is peppered with words carrying violent overtones—*deadline, kill, cut.* Likewise, *burying the lead* has almost zombie-like connotations. The phrase means your most important idea is not located at the beginning of your piece. However, unlike digging in graveyards by lantern light, most buried ideas are hiding in plain sight. They're usually surrounded by other information and thoughts—especially in a first draft. Your job as the editor is to hunt down your lead, move it to the top, and craft a good signpost sentence.

Here's an example of digging up a buried lead. This was my first brain-dump draft of an article I wrote for Better Homes and Garden's *Perennials* magazine in 2007. My pointer sentence was about the subject—the plants in Walt Hodges' garden.

Living Large

Strongly architectural plants bring maturity to a young garden.

Boldly scaled plants with enormous leaves speak of tropical climes not the gray Northwest skies that often hang over this Lake Oswego, Oregon, garden. *Green leafed bananas burst their leaves into pathways, while the orange and red flowers of Canna 'Pretoria' and 'Cleopatra,' nearly as tall as a basketball hoop, march along the lawn. Garden creator Walt Hodges likes to live large and his garden reflects that fondness. His three dogs, whom Walt refers to as "the boys," each weigh well over a hundred pounds. Of course, on his large lot (over two-thirds of an acre) he has to raise a garden of* *out-sized plants. His dogs are big. His backyard is big and the plants he grows there are, well, enormous would not be out of line.*

Okay, I admit, I wrote out my rough draft to see what I was thinking. My first sentence was a reversal idea—*you don't think of the tropics and gray skies together but that's what this gardener has done.* Not very interesting.

After the draft, I constructed my cable-car sentence—In my *feature* about *huge tropical-looking perennials,* I am saying that *Walt Hodges likes everything big—including his garden.*

My slant was created out of the question I asked myself—*why does this garden looks so tropical?* The answer: *this gardener prefers all things huge.* Large leaves look tropical.

Then I noticed the gap. Although the subject was about the big plants, the slant in my cable-car sentence had nothing to do with gray Northwest weather.

So I had to examine that beginning. It didn't support the slant. I went hunting through the draft. I finally dug up the lead and got Walt where he needed to be—right in front. The move also strengthened my title. You'll notice the subhead stayed the same, but now the plant descriptions take second place to Walt and his "boys."

Growing to Extremes

Strongly architectural plants bring maturity to a young garden

Walt Hodges likes living large. *Consider that each of his three enormous dogs—he refers to them as "the boys"—tips the scales at over one hundred pounds. And then there's his oversized back yard in Lake Oswego, Oregon—it extends to almost two-thirds an acre. Given his predilection for all things huge, it makes perfect sense that Hodges would choose boldly scaled perennials with colossal leaves as the signature for his garden. Ten-foot-tall bananas drape their green paddle-shaped leaves into pathways, while the orange and red flow-ers of Canna 'Pretoria' and 'Cleopatra,' nearly as tall as a basketball hoop, march along the lawn.*

Now the lead sees the light of day. I've constructed a signpost sentence that points the way into the article. Please notice the sentence that starts

Given his predilection. It follows my unseen cable-car slant. It's the promise for the whole piece.

There's value in your brain-dump disheveled first drafts. You may dig up exactly what you need to bring your writing to life. Happy hunting.

CHAPTER 11

The Close-Up Edit

Writing Problem: *I don't catch my grammar/spelling/ usage mistakes.*

Rx: *Tackle picky details with these simple suggestions.*

Clean copy is vital. Before anything you write goes out, you've got to hunt down the picky details.

Let's say you create a meme for Facebook, but you misuse a word—SOME DAYS I CAN'T WRITE. I JUST WANT TO *LAY* ON THE BED. Not only will the grammar police notice that it should say "LIE," but even if you manage to avoid them, you still lose a certain credibility. This might not matter too much on social media, but the stakes get higher when you're writing in a more professional setting.

In this chapter, we'll go over easy ways to clean up your copy. After getting into a picky-details mind-set, we'll tackle a quick rundown on punctuation—think of it as traffic control for your writing. The **Write On Exercise: Read Backwards** helps you discover what you've missed. **Cheat Sheets: What's in a Style?, Common Commas**, and **Abuse and Misuse**

of Common Words fill in the gaps. And the **Real-World Review: A Cautionary Tale** helps you see the value of small changes.

How Do You Clean Up Copy?

It makes no difference whether you were taught this stuff or not. It's all right that you can't ever spell *rhythm*. (I can't—my computer changes it for me every time.) These nine steps will help you create a polished piece.

1. Decide It Matters

Shift your mind-set so you push the correction of picky mistakes further up your priority list. We all have priority lists. Even the chronically late will be on time for the terrifying IRS appointment. The important things get pushed up to the top by fear, joy, or necessity. You can do that here.

2. Slow Down

Most of us don't catch a mistake because we're moving too fast through the process. Don't hit that "Send" button. Look again. Give yourself double the time you think you need.

3. Make It a Game

Imagine the hunt for goofs as an interesting game and reward yourself for finding the errors. The editing will get easier. Use the Internet for support. Pick a reliable grammar website and let it be your game partner. Some of my choices are listed in the More Resources section at the back of this book.

4. Turn on Your Spell-Checker

Spell-check corrections aren't perfect. Sometimes they're laughable. Plant names starting with *H* get suggested as *Hitler* more often than I would wish. But turn on your spell-checker at least once during your editing process to make sure you're not missing any major issues. Focus on any highlighted words or phrases, and read the explanations of why they're underlined. If the spelling or word usage isn't obvious, look it up with an online or regular dictionary.

For words that have more than one spelling option (like: *catalog* and *catalogue*), a style guide comes in handy. (See the Cheat Sheet: What's in a Style?) If you've been given a style sheet or you're using a specific style, such as *Chicago Manual of Style* (CMOS) or Associated Press (AP), make that your go-to for questions. Otherwise, rely on the copying process we talked about in Chapter 2. And if you have nothing else to refer to, the suggestions in this chapter will put you on the road to cleaner copy.

5. Read Aloud

You can read a piece out loud to yourself. However, I often notice more if I read it to someone else. They don't have to offer advice. They just have to listen. (I know one writer who presents everything to her dogs; she says they understand every word.)

Reading aloud allows you to check for tone. Are all your sentences on the same place in the tone scale? Or do some veer into the formal, and some go too casual? Reading aloud also gives you the chance to notice sentences that are too long—you run out of breath before you get to the end. You'll also find ones with odd or missing punctuation that messes up your rhythm. You might find words that could be misunderstood—is that verb *read* in present tense or past?

6. Notice Your Darlings

The journalism adage, "Kill your darlings," describes cutting writing you love because it doesn't serve the piece. Reading aloud can help you figure out if you have any darlings, because they're show-offs—they tend to be clever or a bit too funny. They might be puns or odd observations that don't fit. Darlings could be good but inappropriate in the context. Darlings force readers to step back—in admiration or hate—but definitely away from the material.

Defining a darling is subjective. However, here's a hint for spotting them. If every time you read through your piece there's a place you particularly like—but you don't feel that way about the rest of the writing—that word, phrase, or sentence may be a darling. Be hypercritical with these. Ask yourself, *Is it showing off at the expense of what's around it? Could the writing live without it?* Depending on your answer, you might need to cut out a darling.

Every once in a while, darlings can actually point you in a stronger direction. If you like where it's headed, change the writing around the darling to match it. That may mean going all the way back to your slant (Chapter 3).

7. Be Kind to Yourself

The more you delve into the picky details, the more you'll notice your own patterns. Be kind. You're not stupid because you never know whether it's *discreet* or *discrete*. Every time you find an error, you get the chance to teach yourself the correction. Some of it won't stick and that's all right—a surprising amount will. Over time, you're accumulating knowledge. It's your free education. It's okay that you'll always have to look up certain words—or get the computer to automatically change them for you.

8. Get Tough on Typos

Extra spaces, wrong words, extra commas—finding the little buggers is hard. My strategy is to print out material because typos jump out from the page in a way they don't on the screen. But on the computer I hunt for them by enlarging the font. A type size 20 can show up glaring mistakes I miss at 11 or 12.

9. Don't Get Too Hung Up

In a gathering of word nerds, we can fiercely debate punctuation questions. *Does a complete sentence after a colon take a cap on the first word?* Well-thumbed style books get laid on the table like dueling swords. You may discover you like going down grammar rabbit holes. But if not, do your best to be consistent with what you have, and don't worry.

Get Picky on Punctuation

Punctuation is like traffic control. It directs how fast or slow your thoughts come at the reader. It also clarifies how the language is used. Here's a quick run-down.

Speed Controllers

Period

Yes, that's the stop sign. When you read aloud, it's the natural place for a breath. Periods also indicate abbreviations, such as Dr. or esp. You don't need periods in common abbreviations, such as USA. And no, don't add another period after the one on the abbreviation if it ends the sentence.

Informally, periods are used for emphasis. Yes. They. Are.

Question Mark

Question marks are like stopping for a blinking red light. They go at the end of a question. That's about it.

One note: question marks often get lost at the end of long and complex sentences. Go back and cut up the sentence so that a short question is followed by a short statement.

Exclamation Point

These are like the blinking lighted signs over highways, alerting you to traffic conditions. They mean business.

One old-time journalism maxim states, "You have three exclamation points in your lifetime. Use them wisely." Today, especially on social media, whole lifetimes are squandered in one post. That's the style. For other kinds of writing, you rarely need them. You can put exclamation points in a person's quotations to show strong emotion, but not in your opinion or facts. If you find yourself wanting to use one, check your verb. Adding a stronger verb may eliminate your desire for an exclamation point.

Comma

These little guys slow down the traffic, but they don't bring everything to a halt. Consider them like California stops. However, commas get squirrely in lists. Is it *I bought potatoes, beets, and carrots?* Or *potatoes, beets and carrots.* I vote for the first one—called the serial or Oxford comma because it's the most consistently clear. Either way, pick one way and be consistent. See Cheat Sheet: Common Commas for more rules.

Semicolon

Think of semicolons as the hitch that ties truck trailers together. These hooks get used two ways. First, semicolons join two related sentences. It's a way to emphasize the closeness between two complete thoughts. *I packed the picnic hamper with fruit and sandwiches; the wine bottle was tucked on top.* You're showing that the wine and the sandwiches were closely related.

Second, semicolons connect a series of sentences or phrases where you're already using commas. The semicolons make it easier to read:

> *The C-47 was loaded with five hundred bags of seabird guano, which took up the rear cargo area; forty bags of kelp meal, stored near the cockpit; and a shipment of sparkling hula hoops, zip-tied in groups of twenty-five each, which bounced and slid as the plane took off.*

Colon

Think of the colon as a truck's air horn. It blares—*look at this.* You're asking readers to notice a following phrase, sentence, or quotation. Colons tend to show up in more formal writing. Phrases without both a subject and verb don't merit a cap. Colons also serve to introduce a long quotation that is indented in a block. Like an air horn, treat colons with a certain reserve.

Em Dash

These long dashes (—) are very adaptable. They can take the place of parentheses, commas, and colons. When replacing a pair of parentheses with an em dash, you can make your writing more casual and also emphasize the content of the parentheses. They set off thoughts that interrupt the flow—*here's an example*—without overcomplicating the sentence. When replacing a comma, the em dash can help a reader visually parse the sentence more easily. Lastly, em dashes can be used instead of a colon when you want to draw more attention to whatever information follows—*like this*. Unless you're working in AP style, don't add spaces around the em dash.

Even more than colons, em dashes get overused. If you favor them—I do—restrain yourself. Hunt them down and reconsider. A comma or *and* may be fine.

Cheat Sheet: Common Commas

Use commas

- **Between a list or series of items**
  Around the corner came a fire truck, an ambu-lance, and a ladder truck.
  I prefer the serial comma. You might like leaving the last comma off. Be consistent either way.

- **Between adjectives that could be connected with *and***
  I saw a short, agile firefighter.
  If you can put and between the two, you need the comma. If you can't, you don't.
  I saw a large ladder truck.

- **Between two complete thoughts joined by a connecting word**
  I heard the fire truck, but my brother heard the ambulance.
  Without a subject and verb on either side of the connector, no comma.
  I heard the fire truck and the ambulance.

- **After explanatory phrases that start a sentence**
  Before I had breakfast, the fire trucks arrived.
  If the explanatory phrase ends the sentence, you don't need a comma.
  The fire trucks arrived before I had breakfast.

- **To set off words that shift or interrupt the thought**

  The street, however, was blocked with emergency vehicles.

  The words yes and no are also set off with commas.

  No, I didn't need help crossing the street.

- **To set off nonessential phrases or descriptions**

  The neighbor's furniture, which she inherited from her mother, littered the lawn.

  It's nonessential if you can take out the phrase which she inherited from her mother and the meaning stays the same. The neighbor's furniture littered the lawn. An essential phrase is one needed to identify the furniture. Essentials don't need commas.

  The neighbor's furniture from the living room littered the lawn.

- **To set off quotations inside sentences**

  "At least we're all safe," the neighbor said, "and they rescued our dog."

Connectors and Hitches

Apostrophe

This mark declares ownership, like a vehicle registration connects a car and driver—***Phillip's*** *sports car is yellow.* If more than one person owns the thing, the apostrophe goes on the outside of the *s.* *The **brothers'** car often comes in first.* The apostrophe also connects two words as a stand-in for the letter left out—***Don't*** *touch their car.* Numbers left out of year and in numbers and letters by themselves no longer need apostrophes—*Philip bought his car in **58**. He drove around the parking lot in figure **8s** between cones marked with **As** and **Bs**.*

Please note: although the possessive pronoun *its* owns things, it never takes an apostrophe. *The car's best attributes are **its** leather seats and rag top.* Only use the apostrophe for the letter left out. ***It's** a special car.*

Hyphens

These connectors are like small car hitches. They appear when writing out numbers from *twenty-one* to *ninety-nine*. Also, hyphenate with words that start with a capital letter. My favorite—*T-shirt*. Yes, it's always capped unless you spell it out as *tee-shirt*. Think about a T-shirt lying flat on a bed and you'll never be tempted to make it lowercase or unhyphenate it again.

Hyphens also tie two adjectives together. *We were stuck in slow-moving traffic.* Both *slow* and *moving* are adjectives coming ahead of the word *traffic*. The test for whether to hyphenate? Remove one of the adjectives and see if the meaning stays the same. If it does, you don't need a hyphen. If it doesn't, hyphenate. *Stuck in **slow** traffic*, or *stuck in **moving** traffic?* Subtle, but not quite the same meaning. Use the hyphen. This rule is shifting. In the future, you may see far fewer hyphens. In any case, don't hyphenate adverbs, which describe *how* the traffic moved. No hyphen for *We were stuck in slowly moving traffic.*

En Dash

These short dashes (–) are usually used to represent range of numbers, like span of time (1993–1994) or a score (2–3). They can also indicate versus situations (Ducks–Beavers) or when two words have a conflict, connection, or direction (liberal–conservative, east–west). Don't add spaces around the en dash.

Ellipsis

These three dots (...) are like gaps in the road traffic. They indicate something left out. The word *ellipsis* means the set of three. More than one set are called *ellipses*. Let's say you were reviewing a book and you wanted to quote this sentence. "*She wandered down through the carnival midway, past the man hawking cookware, and rounded the corner before she discovered the box."* You'd shorten by taking out the man selling cookware. *"She wandered down through the carnival midway...and rounded the corner before she discovered the box."* But remember, your removal of information shouldn't change the original meaning. If you also took out *and rounded the corner,* she would find the box on the midway, and that's not factually correct.

Ellipses are also used in quotations, to indicate the speaker's words trailing off. *"No, she shouldn't go there,"* he said, *"because the animals are loose...."* If the ellipsis falls at the end of a sentence, a period follows. That indication of thought trailing off has now slid into informal writing, especially in emails.

Big Trucks and Under the Hood

I think of the mechanics in this section as the parts that keep the communication engine running. Just as different cars need different spark plugs, so too mechanics change depending on what style or format you're into. These are just general guidelines.

Quotation Marks

Think of these as specialized word carriers, moving down the highway with the people's speech packed behind the doors, transferred exactly as they said it. (For other uses of quotation marks, check the Cheat Sheet: What's in a Style?)

Quotations are part of sentences. Commas, question marks, and exclamation points are tucked inside. *"Get down off that roof!"* she yelled. *"Just wait until your father gets home."* If the two quotations are part of a whole thought, they would be joined with commas: *"But if you come down right now,"* she said, *"I won't tell him."*

Single quotes show speech inside the quotation marks. *"I just talked to him and he told me, 'I'm bringing raspberry ice cream home.' So you better get down,"* she said. For clarity, when another person speaks, or a different thought begins, start a new paragraph.

Capitals

See the Cheat Sheet: What's in a Style? for an in-depth dive into using capitalizations. Some other considerations: Writing all in caps, or partly in caps for emphasis, is considered shouting or just rude. And capping some words because you think they are important is not a great idea.

Numbers

If you're not sure, spell out numbers up to a hundred. Hyphenate from twenty-one to ninety-nine. Use numerals above that. Editors who don't like it will change it. Unless your writing is extremely informal or you're showing math, don't start any sentence with a numeral. Rework it instead so the number isn't first, or spell the number out. You can use numerals for dates, addresses, scores, fractions, decimals, time of day, and money.

Parentheses

Going back to our road metaphor, what's contained in parentheses is like the sound of electric cars. The information is a whisper. It is incidental or extra. Many readers skip over parentheses. In my garden writing, it's common to put scientific plant names in parentheses—Jacob's ladder (*Polmonium yezoense*). That way, readers don't get hung up on the Latin, but plant enthusiasts can find it. If what you put inside the parentheses is important, you might recast your sentence to get rid of them. One more addition: parentheses go around the acronym the first time you spell out a name. For example, you might write, *I use the* Chicago Manual of Style *(CMOS)*.

Cheat Sheet: What's in a Style?

Italics, quotation marks, and capitalization

A style guide can be your new best friend. Style guides or style sheets are a set of rules for picky details. Standard style guides, such as the *Chicago Manual of Style* (CMOS) or the *Associated Press Stylebook* (AP) can make your life easier by dictating what to do. Others you might come across are from the academic Modern Language Association (MLA) and the American Psychological Association (APA). Or, your company might have a style sheet that says exactly how they want their brand writing handled.

As a reluctant writer, one of the toughest things to handle is that style guides often disagree with each other. For example, CMOS says to italicize the names of movies, and AP puts them in quotes.

Styles are also always in a state of flux. The guides are constantly updated. Don't be discouraged by the changes. It's part of the game.

Now that you know style guides exist, you can find out if one applies to the writing project you need to tackle. However, if you don't have a guide to follow, use this general list for consistency on italics, quotation marks, and capitalization.

Italics
- **Major titles:** names of books, magazines, newspapers, pamphlets, long poems, plays, TV shows, movies, music, dance pieces, visual art, comics, legal cases, software, blogs, podcasts.
- **Specific names of vehicles**: planes, trains, ships, spacecraft
- **Words as words**: including words or phrases in another language
- **Stand-alone letters and numbers**
- **Emphasis**: usually employed in less formal writing

Quotation Marks
- **Minor titles**: names of chapters, essays, articles, short stories, short poems, specific TV and radio episodes
- **Quotes**
- **Sneer quotes**: indicates sarcasm, disdain, irony

Don't use quotation marks for:
- **Religious works**: the name of the Bible, Quran, or the names of divisions inside them
- **Titles**: the name at the top of your own writing

Capitalizations
- **The first word of a sentence, including those inside quotes:** *The hummingbird stops at our window feeder. "Wow," says my little nephew.*
- **Specific people, places, things:** *Our hummingbirds travel all the way from Mexico. My nephew Dan loves them.*
- **Titles of people:** *Margaret Wang, PhD, recommends making hummingbird food only with white sugar.*
- **Important words in titles and subtitles:** *I've read her book,* Hummingbirds of the World—Fierce Flyers on a Long Journey Home.
- **Abbreviations:** departments, government agencies, organizations, corporations, media station call letters, countries, specific time, dates

  Although the EPA does not keep track, I heard on KLCC, my local NPR station, that the use of herbicides is not helping the hummingbird population. My hummers arrive at 4:00 A.M. and don't stop feeding until 7:00 P.M. Examples of sugar-water feeders were found in ancient Egyptian sites dating back to 500 B.C.E.

Verbs Are the Movers and Shakers

We talked about powering up your verbs as a quick-fix in Chapter 9. In your small-scale edit, here are a few more considerations.

Passive Voice

Hats off to whoever came up with the zombie test. If you can add the words *by zombies* to your verb and it makes sense, then you are in the passive voice. *The hedge was clipped (by zombies).* Switch verbs and subjects until the zombies are cast out. Very occasionally, you may want the passive voice. Readers probably don't care that a garden crew from Upsa Daisy clipped the hedge.

Subjunctive

If you've studied a foreign language, you may have run into the past subjunctive tense. It's used to indicate that a situation is contrary to known fact.

However, in English, the past subjunctive has disappeared—except in that ancient *to be* verb. And then, the only awareness of the subjunctive occurs when *was* turns into *were*. In the musical, *Fiddler on the Roof,* Tevya sings, "If I *were* a rich man." That little clue tells me that we have shifted into an unreal world. That's all that's left in English to indicate that mood of longing, reaching into the unknown, and yes, even magic. So let's honor the little remnant by using it when appropriate.

Just remember, not all sentences beginning with *if* move into the subjunctive. Concrete happenings remain with *was*. *If I was singing off key yesterday, I apologize.*

Present or Past?

Verb tenses get confusing in certain situations. For instance, when you are describing the plot of a book, you use the present tense. It's as if the book goes on living in the present, even if it was written long ago. While Mark Twain *wrote The Adventures of Huckleberry Finn* in 1884, Huck *runs* away with Jim in the present tense. The same is true when writing about nature or science. In general, trees or microbes *grow*, present tense. In specific examples of trees or microbes, if you're writing about past events, use past tense.

Another tense issue is whether to use *says* (present) or *said* (past) when quoting someone. If you have no example to follow, think of it this way: are the quotes tied to a scene or circumstance? If so, use past tense *said*. *Last week Lee Lu, chair of the board, stood up in the meeting and said, "We have a broader mission than just the bottom line."* However, if you are taking quotes from an interview with Lee Lu, and using them untethered from a scene or circumstance, use present tense *says*. *The shift in the company's philosophy is reflected in the chair of the board's stance. Lee Lu says, "We have a broader mission than just the bottom line."*

More Picky Details

Here's a collection of observations about common first-draft mistakes I saw repeated over the years. Look for them as you edit your work.

Prepositions Strung Out Like Boxcars

Many of us write long sentences, with prepositional phrases banging around like empty boxcars, rocking and rolling down the line. *On the longest day of summer, we walked up the hill through the dry California grass until, at the top, in the distance, the Pacific Ocean spread out before us as the sun dropped into the sea while at the same time behind our backs the moon rose over the bay.* Whew. That's a long train.

Prepositions are the red flag here, even if length were not an issue— *on, up, through, at, in, before, as, into, behind, over*. Check your prepositions. To simplify, cut your sentences into smaller chunks with fewer words. *We climbed the hill through midsummer dry California grass. The Pacific Ocean spread below us. At sunset, the moon rose behind our backs.* Yes, a certain rhythm gets lost, but the sentences no longer bang and clank like empty boxcars.

Simultaneous Action

In real life, we often experience things simultaneously. The sun drops into the sea at the exact moment the moon rises behind. But when you're writing, it's better to allow the reader to come across incidents in a linear fashion, rather than being bombarded all at once. Check for words like *as*, and *when*, and *at the same time*. Simultaneous presentation can end up as rhythmic, especially when used repeatedly. *As I sat down on the rock, a wasp stung my hand. When I jumped up, it stung me again.* Better to be more Hemingway about it. Remove the *as* and *when*. Let one thing come after the other.

The Problem of *He/She*

Thank you, American Dialect Society (ADS), for naming *they* as Word of the Year for 2015. The humble plural pronoun can now officially be paired up with singular words like *someone, somebody,* and *everybody*. Until recently, to be correct you had to write the always awkward—*Somebody won the office betting pool and he or she needs to collect his or her winnings.* The fix was to recast the sentence—*The person who won the office betting pool needs to collect the winnings.* But now, thanks to the ADS, and the *AP Stylebook* and others, we can write—*Somebody won the office betting pool and they need to collect their winnings.* Hurrah for this nonbinary gender change.

Ghost Quotes

My journalism students were fond of this one. A ghost quote is when you put in a quote, but don't attribute it to a specific person. The quote hangs there, and the reader has to figure out who said it. It might seem obvious in the context of the writing—after all, you were just talking about the CEO—but readers may not jump when you do. Sometimes you can get away with ghost quotes in dialogue where two people are exchanging thoughts. But most times, it's best to attribute.

Specialty Speak

Two bystanders assisted in expediting the extraction of a female child from the truck. Really? Couldn't we just say they broke the truck's window and grabbed the girl? Unless you're writing in an extremely specialized field, work hard to simplify. If you are fond of long words, and you're not writing in an area that calls for them, find a shorter, sharper substitute. Why use *verification* when you mean *proof*? Only put in acronyms when you know all your readers will understand them. And please don't invent acronyms, even if you define them in your writing.

One Sentence, One Thought

William Zinsser, author of the classic *On Writing Well*, was a champion of this idea. In your edit, break up any sentence that contains more than one thought. Your writing will be clearer. You'll also end up with more sentence-length variety.

Unique

This word is nothing but trouble. I learned not to use *unique* from my first seriously cranky editor. But he was right. *Unique* means there's nothing like it. And if that's the case, you're going to have to use more words to explain why and how it is unique. And if that's the case, just use those descriptors and drop *unique*. *Unique* also can't be modified. Nothing is very unique, or more unique. *Unique* just is.

Fudging with Qualifiers

Here's the last quick-edit you can do to strengthen your writing. Go through and check qualifiers and modifiers like *just, maybe, sort of, almost,* and *very*. Are they needed? Sentences are stronger if it either is or it isn't. If you can't say that, could you find a better verb to explain why? *Most people seemed to like these sorts of french fries.* Change and add specifics: *The majority of customers preferred the curly french fries.*

Cheat Sheet: Abuse and Misuse of Common Words

My favorite photo circulating on Facebook is of a sign that reads: "Orgasmic blueberries, $2.95." Someone wrote in the comments, "I'll have what she's having."

For your reference, the Internet has misused word lists that go on for miles. Here are the most common I've come across:

accept—to receive / **except**—to exclude

adverse—unfavorable /**averse**—opposed

affect—to influence / **effect**—to bring about

between—used with two / **among**—used with three or more

amoral—without judgment / **immoral**—against morality

all together—everyone here / **altogether**—entirely

allusion—indirect reference / **illusion**—not real impression

capital—a city, money, or letter form / **capitol**—building for lawmakers

cite—to quote / **site**—a place

elicit—to bring up / **illicit**—illegal

eminent—distinguished / **imminent**—about to happen

farther—use with distances / **further**—use with quantities

fewer—use with specific amounts / **less**—use with general quantities

imply—to suggest / **infer**—to conclude

loose—not tight / **lose**—Misplace or not win

percent—use with specific numbers / **percentage**—use with general quantities

sensual—dealing with physical gratification / **sensuous**—pleasing to the senses

that—no comma before the phrase it starts / **which**—the phrase is set off with a comma

to—connects / **too**—as well as / **two**—the number

Words Your Spell-Checker Might Miss

A few word-use conundrums pop up repeatedly in my students' writing. Check to see if your writing has any of these.

- **all right vs. alright:** Sorry, but the first one is correct. You might use (and see) the second spelling in casual writing, but it's not all right (yet).
- **a lot vs. alot:** Again, the first is the way to go. The second spelling is not recognized—but it often shows up in online communications.
- **couldn't care less vs. could care less:** When you say, "I couldn't care less," you're telling people you have no more feelings regarding the subject. You're done. The second means the opposite. You still have a ways to go before arriving at not caring.
- **lectern vs. podium:** *Podium* is substituted for *lectern* so often that some dictionaries are now accepting it as standard. However, in the interest of honoring word ancestries, let's get it right. *Lectern* derives from the Latin verb to read—*leggere*. *Podium* comes from the Latin for foot—*pes, pedis*. All kinds of foot words like *pedestrian* and *podiatrist* come from *pes*. Once you know the histories, it's easy to picture lecterns holding the notes speakers will read. Or you can picture speakers clutching lecterns while their feet stand on the raised platform—the podium.
- **regardless vs. irregardless:** Irregardless sounds more important, right? Wrong. My students used *irregardless* regardless of the number of times I circled it on papers. Regardless means having less regard. If you put in *ir-* in front, you now have not less regard, or a double negative.
- **set vs. sit, lay vs. lie:** Try the peculiar, but effective, egg/bed test. In the present tense, *set* and *lay* need objects—in this case, eggs. *Today I set an egg on the*

bed. Today I lay an egg on the bed. The other verbs *sit* and *lie* never need eggs. *Today I sit on the bed. Today I lie on the bed.* Now, hang in there for yesterday. *Yesterday I set an egg on the bed. Yesterday I laid an egg on the bed.* All good. Remove the eggs. *Yesterday I sat on the bed.* But here's the stumbler: *Yesterday I <u>lay</u> on the bed.* Unfair. How can *lay* be in both places? It's ruled by tense. Combine it with eggs in the present. Use it without eggs in the past. Got it?

If eggs and beds don't help, use these verbs as red flags and always check a verb list.

Write On Exercise: Read Backwards

Time: Depends on length of writing

One of the best methods to discover mistakes is to read in a way that is not your usual pattern.

Step 1. Start at the end. Go to the end of your piece and read each individual word in a single sentence from the period on back. Check for punctuation and spellings. Circle any issues you run into.

Step 2. Read out loud. Now read that same sentence in the normal order. Mark places where you stumble or run out of breath.

Step 3. Repeat. Go through Steps 1 and 2 for each sentence in your piece or section.

Step 4. Make corrections. When you arrive at the beginning, go back and make corrections for anything you circled. On examination, certain boggles may need to be rewritten to solve the problem.

Now Let It Go

When you arrive at the end of the picky details, you've also arrived at the end of your writing journey. If you've discovered tips in this book you can use, and applied the advice as best you can, your writing is good enough. Move on. At the end of a project, many reluctant writers experience an anxiety flash that fosters procrastination. If this happens to you, think about this saying: *Perfect is the enemy of done.*

Done is what you want—nobody needs perfection. Unless you can manage to wriggle out of it, you'll be facing more writing in the future. You'll have another chance to get it right. While that might still make your heart heavy, I hope at this point you can regard your writing process with less reluctance.

Real-World Review: A Cautionary Tale
Journalist Randy Dotinga talks about dealing with the picky details.

If you ever need motivation for not overlooking this final editing step, just go talk to a seasoned reporter. They work on tight deadlines, so it's not always easy to catch mistakes. With that in mind, let me introduce Randy Dotinga.

Randy's a freelance journalist and past president of the American Society of Journalists and Authors (ASJA). I met him at the ASJA's annual meeting in New York several years ago. His good humor in a tough business always shines through. He's been kind enough to share some of his in-the-trenches experiences.

Q. What's the most important thing to remember when dealing with picky details?

A. Be prepared to make mistakes. When I was starting out as a journalist, I agonized over making errors. And I thought I was the only one. A few months ago, I was talking to a fellow journalist who was a newspaper reporter in the 1990s. She told me about sleepless nights worrying over whether she got a fact right. It was stunning for me to find out that I wasn't the only one who obsessed over a possible mistake. I can remember going to a Rolling Stones concert and ruining the entire evening by fretting over a story I'd filed earlier—had I inadvertently promoted a deputy city attorney to city attorney? Turned out the paper held the story for a day, so I had time to check my work.

And remember, even though a mistake may make you feel terrible, especially when you're starting out, the chances are good that it will soon be forgotten. And even the most experienced journalists make mistakes. They misspell names, make assumptions that aren't true, and misquote people. Just check the corrections section in *The New York Times*. Every day they always have multiple corrections because even the best aren't perfect.

Q. Do you have any advice for avoiding errors?

A. The biggest danger is assuming. As far as I can remember, every single mistake I've ever made happened because I assumed something was true. Whenever you mention a fact in your writing you haven't confirmed, think to yourself, "How do I know this?"

Q. Do you have strategies for checking facts?

A. I often get into a writing groove and don't stop to double-check facts because I want to keep going. To remind myself to go back to them, I bold the sentences. Or I'll write something like CHECK THIS. (Although be careful, because you may leave those comments in the story by accident, and then they might get published.)

Q. How do you go back and repair?

A. The Internet has really changed things in terms of correcting articles. These days, you can go online and immediately fix errors in stories. If you're writing for a web-only publication, the initial batch of readers—the ones who read the story before you caught the error—will probably never even know that you screwed up. Corrections are more obvious in print publications.

Q. Okay, Randy, what was your worst picky-detail goof?

A. Back in the early 1990s, I was a rookie reporter at a weekly newspaper in La Jolla, a wealthy neighborhood of San Diego. I got assigned to write about the 50-year celebration of a landmark restaurant on the beach, the Marine Room. It was owned by the Kelloggs, one of the richest and most respected families in town. At one point, I asked our society editor if the Kelloggs were part of the breakfast cereal empire. Yup, she replied. So

I put that into the story without bothering to confirm it. How could the nice lady who covered soirées at the garden club be wrong?

The newspaper came out. The cover of the features section was filled with stories by me about the Marine Room restaurant. I arrived at work to find my editor in snap-crackle-and-pop mode. The La Jolla Kelloggs were not related to the Battle Creek Kelloggs, and they *hated* it when people assumed they were. To make matters worse, our publisher informed my boss that she regularly played tennis with one of the Kelloggs. Game, set, and awkward!

My editor pulled me into his office to scream at me. After a break, for good measure, he yelled at me some more. But I kept my job, barely. This remains the biggest mistake of my journalism career, and I've given Corn Flakes the stink eye ever since.

One Final Point: You Are Not Your Writing

Through the years, I've taught a lot of reluctant writers—a surprising number of them majoring in journalism. Many students wanted to do anything and everything—film, programming, photography—except writing. I've noticed that sometimes the reluctance comes from the painful feeling that if the writing comes up short, so does the writer.

So here's the last thing I want to share with you. For all the writing you must produce—none of it is you. It has your ideas, of course, and whatever craft and skill you bring to it. But it's not the real you, any more than a blob of clay that turns into a lovely bowl on the potter's wheel is the potter. If the writing is clumsy, that's not you. Or if you create a nifty sentence that soars—that's still not you. It's an important distinction, because it allows you to take critique impersonally. You don't ever need to beat yourself up about writing.

The more you take on the know-how and the proficiency of the process, the more you'll see that improving at writing is the same as learning any other pursuit. The more you do it, the better you are. So the most important skill you can develop is your willingness to keep going.

It's as simple as that.

CHAPTER 12

Help Yourself by Helping Someone Else

Writing Problem: *My writing isn't improving fast enough.*
Rx: *Try a group.*

Now that we've finished the steps of the writing process, here's one more way you improve your writing: help someone else. Meeting with another to work on your writing together is a powerful tool. Focus on problems that aren't your own; you have emotional distance. Give feedback to someone else and you raise awareness of your own work. Observe how others tackle a problem and you'll see different ways to think. Meeting regularly can also jump-start your writing process, so you finish before the deadline.

Writers' groups come in all shapes, sizes, and configurations. Some are dedicated to a specific genre of writing, like memoir or mystery. Other groups welcome a mix. Some are open to newcomers. Others have been closed for years. A few require criteria for joining—like published work—but others cater to beginners. In some groups, members create writing at the meetings. Or in some, members bring prepared material and invite critique. Groups meet once a week or once a month or everything in between.

I've been part of a writing group for almost 20 years. We started with very little except an ambition to get better. Over the years, the members have produced five books, hundreds of magazine articles, and countless columns. We're working professionals and we still learn from each other every week. My group has been vital to me.

But—and there's a big *but* here—one premise underlies almost all writing groups, including mine: the people who join them *want* to write. And most reluctant writers don't. Why spend *more* time on something you dislike? I will give you one good reason: writing groups make the act of writing easier. So why not form a reluctant writers' group?

Ten Steps to Set Up a Writing Group

Let's walk through the sequence of forming a new writing group. With each of these steps, I've included my own experience as an example.

1. Two People Make a Group

There might already be writing groups in your area that you can join. But often, starting your own is the easiest, least intimidating option—you can connect with other reluctant writers who are at the same stage as you. And you don't need a ton of people to create a group. In fact, it may be better to start small. If you find one person who can look at your writing and you reciprocate, that's a group.

Our Story: Almost twenty years ago, I took a writing class at my local community college—"Magazine Writing That Sells." I joked that this was opposed to that other class—"Magazine Writing You Keep in Your Closet." After the semester ended, a fellow student and I petitioned the instructor for an ongoing class. Not possible, he said. But he suggested the two of us meet anyway. So we decided to see what we could do by ourselves.

2. Look for Commonality

With a prospective writing buddy, it helps to have something in common. Maybe you both work in the same field. Or you took a workshop together. Or you share the same writing goal. Or, one easy commonality—you've both read this book.

Our Story: For the two of us, we had both taken that original magazine class. Later we used that same class to recruit more members. That way, we were all exposed to the same information.

3. Make Formal Agreements

This may seem silly when you're talking to one other potential writing partner, but for a successful outcome, creating a formal agreement is important (see Steps 4, 5, and 6 for what to include). You don't need to type it out on fancy letterhead or anything—you just need to get your conclusions on paper.

Our Story: The two of us met one morning at a coffee shop. Customers banged out tunes on an old piano in the corner. Over the din, we discovered we both considered ourselves writers, even though our accomplishments in the field were slim. And writers write. So we got out our notebooks—neither of us owned a laptop—and jotted down what we wanted for our meetings—starting with our goal for our group.

4. Decide on a Shared Goal

A shared goal could be something as simple as polishing your writing through editing. Or maybe you might want to get together to do the exercises in this book. Or to help each other finish specific projects.

Treat this step thoughtfully. Right away you'll see whether your goals match up with your future writing buddy's. You can use the Write On Exercise to find out answers. If the goals don't align, well, you've had a nice conversation. Go look for another prospect.

Our Story: Neither of us had ever started a group. But from my experience serving on a nonprofit board, I knew that the clearer the founding goal, the easier to bring it into reality. So we picked a goal: *To help each other make money writing.*

5. Measure for Results

The next step is figuring out how you'll know if you're making progress. What are your expectations? You could ask, What would improved writing look like? Would it mean you'd write in a shorter time? Or with less angst? Or fewer typos? Obviously, finishing a project is a specific result. A clear goal is sharpened by the results you're looking for. That keeps you on task.

You may want to set an introductory time—say, six weeks—after which you evaluate whether meeting together is working or not. If not, part friends. If it's working, make a longer run at it and assess again.

Our Story: We chose to help each other make money because that would mean we were professionals, a result we both wanted. We didn't set a timeline on this, but within six months, we had both gotten well-paid writing work. We were delighted and surprised.

6. Decide on Details

Now you need to nail down the logistics to support your goal. Talk through details like:

- **Group Name:** Will your group have a name?
- **Meeting Location:** Where will you meet? If you want to keep a low profile, perhaps you can snag a meeting room at work on a regular basis without others noticing. Or meet in the corner of the cafeteria. Or maybe over the phone.
- **Frequency and Length:** How often will you meet? How long will your meetings be?
- **Process:** What will the process be for each meeting? How will you offer critique? Will you be obligated to bring something to share every time? Will you take turns leading? Or will all members have parity? (Check out pages 206–209 for more ideas on shaping your critique process.)
- **Sharing Method:** If you're working on printed copies, who will do the printing? Will you send the other person your writing ahead of the meeting, or will you print out your own material to bring in and share? Alternatively, will you use an online program like Google Docs to share on a screen and make edits in real time?

Our Story: We gave our two-person group a name that felt bigger than we were—The Editorial Board. Because neither of us had full-time jobs, we chose Wednesday mornings and met for a maximum of three hours. This time became sacrosanct.

We agreed to work in a public space rather than our homes. Eventually we left the pounding piano players and ended up at a local bookstore, a huge space surrounded by towering bookshelves, whose owner welcomed several working writers' groups.

Each week we resolved to bring material. At first, because we had no actual work, we brought in pitch letters. The two of us formulated the query structure that appears in Chapter 6 because I didn't want to reinvent the wheel every time I had an idea.

7. Consider Areas of Focus

You and your writing buddy don't have to have the same focus. I know of successful groups where everyone writes children's books. In others, the writing mix is both fiction and nonfiction, as well as short pieces and long books. However, most reluctant writers are working on some form of nonfiction. One of you may be rewriting the employee handbook and the other works in marketing. The kind of writing may not be as important as the choice of a similarly inclined writing partner. It's your call.

Our Story: The Editorial Board didn't mean to end up as all nonfiction writers. Frankly, at first we didn't think about it. It just worked out that way. However, we all have different areas of expertise—from gardening and business, to technology and activism. Bonus perk: through the years, I've learned an enormous amount about the others' subjects.

8. Grow the Group

Two people might be the perfect size for your group. Or, at some point, you may want to add more. If you do, concentrate on shared aims. If you use this book as a basis, encourage prospective members to read it first. Explain your group's goal. Sometimes, in the enthusiasm of joining, the goal is overlooked. But a clear objective allows members to leave without hard feelings if their goals don't jive with the group's. You may want to set a trial time period and then reassess on all sides. Also, be aware that as you grow bigger, you may have to change your working process.

Our Story: The two of us went back to the class the following semester. We found two more members, one of whom had actually published in a magazine. The four of us made up the core group.

At one point, the numbers rose to seven. That was too big. With only three hours, it was a scramble to get to everyone's work each week.

However, several participants chose to leave when it became clear that their objectives differed from The Editorial Board's. One person was seeking self-actualization through her writing. Another was processing a terrible grief by writing about her loss. Nothing wrong with those aims, but in both cases, the Board's stated goal of making money functioned as it should. The would-be members recognized that publishing for pay was not their foremost objective. Since then, new members have joined us.

9. Examine Unstated Group Norms

Even if you write down your plans in the beginning, many group dynamics remain unsaid and unwritten. For instance, notice patterns in your meetings. Do you tend to concede to only one person's expertise? Do you make unspoken judgments about other's work? Do you hold back for fear of being judged? Or do you have expectations for the group that are not being met?

It's important to be aware of these hidden areas. Like frost cracks in a rock, they are the lines along which a group can split. Every organization has them. But I think the secret to longevity is to notice the unsaid dynamics and deal with them as best you can with respect for all the members. If you're on the lookout, issues can often be deflated before they carry a lot of emotional weight.

It also helps to allow for other people's foibles, as long as they don't interfere with the process. Over the years, people who know each other tend to become more forgiving of familiar traits. If instead you find yourself becoming more irritated, either try for a fix, or call it a day and part company on reasonable terms. If a group stops serving you, it's time to move on with grace.

Our Story: In all the years The Editorial Board has been meeting, we've only had one major blow up that resulted in a member leaving. Now looking back, I understand the argument was about unspoken expectations on one person's part that exceeded the group members' ability (or willingness) to meet them.

As the years have gone by, some of our group norms have shifted. We started out being polite and never over-talking each other. But now we can finish each other's thoughts. It may be to our detriment, but over-talking has become standard. Sometimes we simply dive into a critique, one after the other, without waiting our turns. But usually, at a certain point, one of us will call it. Then we'll all back off and try to be more respectful.

10. Create a Safe Space

Finally, safety is the secret to a successful group. Google recently announced the results of a five-year study, the Aristotle Project, that looked at the question of why some groups were productive and some were not. They found that successful groups create clear goals and foster a culture that allows people to depend on each other. But, the most important aspect according to Charles Duhigg (writing in the *New York Times Magazine*, 2/25/16), is feeling psychologically safe in the group. He says, "In the best teams, members listen to one another and show sensitivity to feelings and needs."

Our Story: Without knowing any of that, The Editorial Board managed to institute a critique process that reflects Google's findings. We tried to take turns and give each person equal time. We set up a system for criticism that allows for us to give positive as well as negative feedback without too much emotional freight. We encouraged a group norm that everyone's opinion about the writing has equal importance. We attempted not to argue over differing advice. We supported the known strengths of the members.

We've also created traditions. For example, when one of us scores an important gig, we take the others out for breakfast. Sometimes we'll bring back a published piece for a show and tell. And signed books are always brought as gifts for fellow members.

Write On Exercise: Make Sharing Ideas the Goal

Time: Ten minutes

You can do this exercise with a potential writing partner. Spend a few minutes answering the questions in a timed writing. If your first answers aren't detailed enough, rinse and repeat the whole exercise.

Step 1. Why do I want to set up a group? (60 seconds)

Step 2. What do I want out of a group? (60 seconds)

Step 3. How would my goals in the group be realized? (45 seconds)

Step 4. Name the goal of your prospective group. (10 seconds)

Step 5. Share and compare. After the writing, share and compare the answers with your partner. Are the responses similar? If not, is there a way to tweak them to come up with a common goal?

Step 6. Write out your conclusion together.

The Editorial Board's Working Critique Process

Sharing your work with a writing buddy involves critique—both giving and taking it. Criticism is tough. It's tough to take, and it's tough to give. So what's the best way to go about it?

Finding a style that functions for you and your partner may take trial and error. There's the sandwich delivery—layer something critical between two statements of cheer. There's the "I message," which is supposed to take away the sting—"I get confused when you start all your sentences the same way." Then there's the gruff-editor position—marking up another person's writing and handing it back. What doesn't work is the nice-nice approach, where someone is too kind (or too scared) to offer advice. That doesn't help them, and it doesn't help you.

The Editorial Board uses a functional critique process—detailed on the following pages. It allows a certain emotional distance from the material. It has kept us from stepping (too hard) on each other's toes for all these years. While your specific goal as a reluctant writer may not be the same as ours, the method for conducting critique could be the same.

We gather around a table in the bookstore. Each writer brings enough printouts for the other members. In the interest of time, we may have to submit only part of a long piece. Everyone makes notes on the copies and then the writer gathers them back up. We used to put our names on them, but now we recognize each other's handwriting and favorite pens.

1. The Group's Goal Is Foremost

The goal for your group rules the critique. In our case, we focus our feedback on what will make the writing saleable.

2. The Writer Asks for Objectives

Before a reading, the writer may ask for specifics from the others. Different pieces may be at various stages of completion. One might need an overall edit. Another could use ideas for cutting the word count. If it's a very rough draft, the writer could ask for help discovering the main thread.

3. The Writer Reads the Pages Aloud

Reading aloud helps define rhythms, sort out sentence length, and generally see whether ideas are getting across. The others listen and mark down notations. (Remember, a paper covered with arrows and lines is a good thing!) The observations fall into one of three categories.

- **Velcros stick:** Velcros are the memorable items, the things that stick in your mind. In our group we tend to draw stars or exclamation points next to these. This positive feedback is not just for ego stroking. Most writers never know what moves a reader; this is valuable information. It's important to find out your strengths—whether it's powerful verbs or pointer sentences that rock. Discovering Velcros week after week plays a big a role in learning. And giving Velcros to others helps you tune in to what makes writing work.

- **Bobbles (aka boggles) stumble:** We use the words *bobble* and *boggle* interchangeably to describe points where the material falters or gets confusing. Bobbles might be anything from a big-concept idea that never made it onto the page, or simple grammar mistakes, misspellings, and typos. Anything is fair game as long as it fits what the writer has asked for. For instance, we don't do a picky-edit on a piece that's clearly in line for a massive overhaul. We save that feedback for when writing needs a quick polish.
- **Fixes make it better:** The last markups are about suggestions for ways to improve. If a person notes a bobble, there's an obligation to offer a fix. And if there's one thing I've learned through working in a group, it's that bobbles can be solved in countless ways. The more suggestions a writer gets, the better.

4. The Members Take Turns Delivering Critique

We focus on Velcros first. Then hit the bobbles. We never comment, "I don't like this." Instead we explain *why* we bobbled. It's better to say, "I had to read this sentence twice to understand it." And then offer a fix. If you are working with a partner who gets stumped on the fix, try brainstorming solutions together. In a larger group, if one person can't think of a fix, it's opened to the others. They might all agree, or have widely differing observations. Each person is free to offer any solution without judgment from the other members. There's no best fix. Yes, some might prove more elegant, but that's up to the writer to decide.

5. The Writer Receives the Critique Without Argument

Because the writer is ultimately in charge of changes, there's no need to say anything. One exception: If the writer feels that the person giving the critique has missed the point, they may say, "I was trying to say this..." and then state the idea. Often that thought has not yet made it clearly to the paper. That's the cue for other members to grab their pens and copy down the writer's words. By speaking aloud, the writer may discover a better way to get to the point. The group can help by taking dictation.

6. Don't Argue Over Whose Critique Is Right

We don't disagree—most times—about another member's solution, even if it's radically opposed to the one we hold. That practice helps everyone leave their egos at the door. If an issue comes up about how something should be done, we defer to the specific style the writer is using.

7. The Writer Decides

It's up to the writer to take each critique and decide what will be used or thrown away. The only caution here—don't decide to do nothing. In our group, we assume that if another member has noticed it, you should be deal with it one way or another. The members of our group rarely know how the writing problems get solved, unless a piece is brought in again. The group's support builds confidence, but the writer is always in charge.

Why It Works

I remember a journalism professor lifting his eyebrows in horror over peer-led learning, because he'd found, "Students are so often wrong." He felt untrained peers could lead a group down a very bad rabbit hole. Students needed someone highly skilled—like himself—to teach them.

Maybe. But it's been my experience that most people recognize good writing when they see it. They might not know why it's good, but they can tell. And in a group—when you gather more than one opinion in feedback and use various methods for problem-solving—everyone's writing improves.

With group learning, when you're called upon to help another, you're actively engaged. You're not passively collecting pearls of wisdom. Sure, you receive helpful suggestions from your partner, but far more importantly, you attempt to solve your partner's problems. You begin to see how to do that on a regular basis. That in turn alerts you to your own challenges. You create patterns for how to upgrade the material. You discover your strengths.

If writing is your challenge, I hope you'll take a chance on a group. And if the first one doesn't work out, just keep going. Find another partner. You don't have to travel the writing road alone.

RESOURCES

The writing world is full of more guides to get you where you need to go.

On my own writing path, I've found the following resources to be useful—but this list is certainly not definitive. These suggestions are simply part of the vast collection of writing books and websites waiting for you after you've walked through the *Write Better Right Now* gateway.

While most of the books are available to buy online, I recommend going to a bookstore and perusing the offerings. Look at the typeface, smell the pages, see which one appeals to you. Whether you're searching for a book that's specific to your line of work, or want another overview guide, I hope you'll find inspiration and support for your writing journey.

Practical Advice

The Book on Writing: The Ultimate Guide to Writing Well, Paula LaRocque, Grey & Guvnor Press, 2003. This book has been around a long time, but it covers all the bases. Ms. LaRocque weaves real-life writing examples into every chapter.

Harvard Business Review Guide to Better Business Writing, Bryan A. Garner, Harvard Business Review Press, 2013. If you're writing for any kind of business, go here. This book is from the man who convinces lawyers to write in plain English. Bad writing examples and their fixes are a hallmark.

Heads You Win!: An Easy Guide to Better Headline and Caption Writing, Paul LaRocque, Marion Street Press, 2003. Working with headlines and captions can focus your thinking. This skinny book demystifies the process.

Help! For Writers: 210 Solutions to the Problems Every Writer Faces, Roy Peter Clark, Little, Brown and Company, 2013. This book is all about problem-solving. Mr. Clark's solutions are always grounded in useful ideas and techniques.

The Hook: How to Share Your Brand's Unique Story to Engage Customers, Boost Sales, and Achieve Heartfelt Success, Richard Krevolin, Career Press, 2015. Mr. Krevolin details the art of adding storytelling to all kinds of business writing.

How to Write It: A Complete Guide to Everything You'll Ever Write, Sandra E. Lamb, Ten Speed Press, 2011. You want examples to copy? This friendly reference guide gives writing examples for every situation. This one's so valuable, it's right up there on my shelf with the dictionary.

How to Write Short: Word Craft for Fast Times, Roy Peter Clark, Little, Brown and Company, 2014. Writing short is always harder than writing long. This is one of many books Mr. Clark has turned out, loaded with great ideas and tips.

It Was the Best of Sentences, It Was the Worst of Sentences: A Writer's Guide to Crafting Killer Sentences, June Casagrande, Ten Speed Press, 2010. If your sentences tend toward the incomprehensible, read this.

Microstyle: The Art of Writing Little, Christopher Johnson, W. W. Norton & Company, 2012. Another book about packing the most into the smallest amount of writing. Mr. Johnson makes it look easy with solid advice.

On Writing Well: The Classic Guide to Writing Nonfiction (30th Anniversary Edition), William Zinsser, Collins (imprint of HarperCollins), 2006. Mr. Zinsser mixes inspiration and practicality with style. This book is one of my favorites.

The Renegade Writer: A Totally Unconventional Guide to Freelance Writing Success, Linda Formichelli and Diana Burrell, Marion Street Press Inc., 2005. Most reluctant writers, by their very nature, aren't freelancers. But the strategies in this book are useful if you have to get your writing out in the world.

Sin and Syntax: How to Craft Wickedly Effective Prose, Constance Hale, Three Rivers Press, 2013. This book features solid advice presented with a light touch.

Story Craft: The Complete Guide to Writing Narrative Nonfiction, Jack Hart, University of Chicago Press, 2012. This is it. If you have a story that must be written, look here. Mr. Hart turns practical advice and great examples into their own compelling narrative.

The Subversive Copy Editor: Advice from Chicago, Carol Fisher Saller, University of Chicago Press, 2016. When you're cleaning up your own copy, you are an editor—so this book's a good fit. Many excellent ideas in here will give you an overview of the process.

When Good People Write Bad Sentences: 12 Steps to Better Writing Habits, Robert W. Harris, St. Martin's Press, 2004. It's basic, it's down-to-earth, and it works.

A Writer's Coach: The Complete Guide to Writing Strategies That Work, Jack Hart, Anchor Books, 2007. There are only a few books where I would say, "Read this and you *will* be a better writer." This is one. When you're ready, open this book for a great reading and writing ride.

A Writer's Guide to Nonfiction, Elizabeth Lyon, Perigee Books, 2003. The description on the cover says it all—this book's a "clear, practical reference for all writers of essays, memoirs, biographies, how-to, self-help, technical, features, articles, profiles, Q&A, travel, food/recipes, outdoor, and nature." I find the summation lists at the ends of chapters to be especially useful.

Grammar and Style

But, Can I Start a Sentence with "But?": Advice from the Chicago Style Q&A, The University of Chicago Press Editorial Staff, 2016. The University of Chicago team has got the answers to grammar and style questions you might not have thought about—but should.

The Curious Case of the Misplaced Modifier: How to Solve the Mysteries of Weak Writing, Bonnie Trenga, Writer's Digest, 2008. You're a detective on the case of bad writing. This book's a fun read that makes a typically tedious topic—grammar—actually enjoyable.

Woe Is I: The Grammarphobe's Guide to Better English in Plain English, Patricia T. O'Conner, Riverhead Books, 2010. Grammar explained in the best way—with humor.

Under the Grammar Hammer: The 25 Most Important Grammar Mistakes and How to Avoid Them, Douglas Cazort, CreateSpace Independent Publishing Platform, 2014. I've had this one on my shelf since 1992. It's a skinny book, concise and easy to read. Mr. Cazort's explanations are terrific.

Exercises

The Writer's Idea Book: How to Develop Great Ideas for Fiction, Nonfiction, Poetry and Screenplays, Jack Heffron, Writer's Digest Books, 2012. Most reluctant writers already know what they must write about. If not, here's a book of prompts that will launch your ideas.

Now Write! Nonfiction: Memoir, Journalism, and Creative Nonfiction Exercises from Today's Best Writers and Teachers, Sherry Ellis, Jeremy P. Tarcher/Penguin, 2009. The exercises in here range from the pragmatic to the fanciful and everything in between.

Writing Down the Bones: Freeing the Writer Within, Natalie Goldberg, Shambhala, 2016. While Ms. Goldberg has a series of these books, the first one—written back in pre-personal computer days—still remains the best for getting you on the free-write bandwagon.

Borrowed From Fiction

How to Write a Movie in 21 Days: The Inner Movie Method, Viki King, HarperCollins, 1993. I know, the last thing a reluctant writer thinks about is writing a movie script. But this book outlines dramatic structure so clearly you can borrow it for all kinds of writing. It also shows you how to organize a long project into a short time.

Plot & Structure: Techniques and Exercises for Crafting a Plot That Grips Readers from Start to Finish, James Scott Bell, Writer's Digest Books, 2004. This book has good ideas about the basic building blocks of writing you can transfer to your nonfiction projects.

Story Structure Architect: A Writer's Guide to Building Dramatic Situations and Compelling Characters, Victoria Lynn Schmidt, Writer's Digest Books, 2005. Here are fifty-five structures that could be used for your own nonfiction storytelling.

Wired for Story: The Writer's Guide to Using Brain Science to Hook Readers from the Very First Sentence, Lisa Cron, Ten Speed Press, 2012. While this book offers fiction examples, the brain science Ms. Cron cites is applicable to nonfiction writing as well.

Inspiration

Good Prose: The Art of Nonfiction, Tracy Kidder and Richard Todd, Random House Trade Paperbacks, 2013. If you want to read about writing, stick your nose in this book and get inspired.

The Wave in the Mind: Talks and Essays on the Writer, the Reader, and the Imagination, Ursula K. LeGuin, Shambhala Publications, 2004. These are the divine Ms. LeGuin's observations on a wide range of worthwhile subjects connected in some way to the act of writing.

On Writing: A Memoir of the Craft, Stephen King, Scribner, 2010. Stephen King's thoughts and musings on life as a writer, interlaced with insightful advice.

Group Work

Toxic Feedback: Helping Writers Survive and Thrive, Joni B. Cole, University Press of New England, 2006. While aimed at fiction writers, the issue of handling critique—both taking and giving it—makes this a good choice.

Writing without Teachers, Peter Elbow, Oxford University Press, 1998. With a 25th anniversary edition in 1998, this book's been around a long time. Few others address the subject of self-guided learning so well. Mr. Elbow knows it inside and out.

Specialized Writing

21st Century Feature Writing, Carla Johnson, Pearson, 2004. Take a deep dive into formats you can use for all kinds of writing—not just features.

The Art and Craft of Feature Writing: Based on The Wall Street Journal Guide, William E. Blundell, Emerald Group Publishing, 1988. This book is a classic aimed at journalists. However, the step-by-step approach can be used with many different types of writing.

The Art of Feature Writing: From Newspaper Features and Magazine Articles to Commentary, Earl R. Hutchison, Oxford University Press, 2007. Any book whose preface opens with "Thank you for reading these sentences," is a book you can learn from. It's long and thorough and worth your time.

Art-Write: The Writing Guide for Visual Artists, Vicki Krohn Amorose, Luminaire Press, 2013. Ms. Amorose's step-by-step approach and helpful writing advice extends far beyond the artist's statement into marketing and promotion. That makes it a useful read for those in other fields.

The Craft of Revision, Donald Murray, Cengage Learning, 2003. Squarely targeted at journalism students, this book's packed with solid editing information that anyone can use.

The Everyday Writer, Andrea A. Lunsford, Bedford/St. Martin's, 2016. This is my favorite go-to for academic writing. It's tabbed for easy referral, covers many styles, and goes over all the basics.

Feature Writing for Newspapers and Magazines: The Pursuit of Excellence, Edward Jay Friedlander and John D. Lee, Mysearchlab Series for Communication, 2010. This is a classic journalism textbook, but the work here is easy to understand if you want to teach yourself the basics.

How to Blog a Book: Write, Publish and Promote Your Work One Post at a Time, Nina Amir, Amazon Digital Service, 2014. Even if authoring a book is not your goal, the information on writing is handy, especially if your job demands you write a blog.

How to Write and Give a Speech: A Practical Guide for Anyone Who Has to Make Every Word Count by Joan Detz, St. Martin's Press, 4th edition, 2014. Even if you were never called upon to give a speech, your writing would still be better because Ms. Detz's approach is so clear and concise. It includes tips for how to plan ahead for any last-minute challenges.

How to Write Copy That Sells: The Step-by-Step System for More Sales, to More Customers, More Often, Ray Edwards, Morgan James Publishing, 2016. If you have to use your writing to sell anything, this book contains an insider's view of the practicalities.

The Only Grant Writing Book You'll Ever Need, Ellen Kaush and Arlen Sue Fox, Basic Books, 2014. If you're faced with this particular writing challenge, the title says it all.

The Situation and the Story: The Art of Personal Narrative, Vivian Gornick, Farrar, Straus and Giroux, 2002. Check out this book if you want to know about writing from a personal point of view.

Web Copy That Sells: The Revolutionary Formula for Creating Killer Copy That Grabs Their Attention and Compels Them to Buy, Maria Veloso, AMACOM, 2013. As a reluctant writer, you may find yourself in need of advice on how to sell a product or service through writing. The style is intense, but the advice is sound.

Writing and Reporting News: A Coaching Method, Carole Rich, Cengage Learning, 2012. Reluctant writers will rarely find themselves reporting. However, this textbook contains so much important information, it's worth a look.

Writing Research Papers: A Complete Guide, James D. Lester and James D. Lester, Jr., Pearson, 2015. With this book, a son carries on the legacy of his father's work for definitive coverage of writing academic research papers.

Reference

Depending on your writing projects, you may need a variety of reference books or style guides. Here are a few of the most common.

The American Heritage Dictionary on the English Language, Houghton Mifflin Harcourt, 2016. If any dictionary can turn you into a word nerd, this is it.

The Associated Press Stylebook and Briefing on Media Law, The Associated Press, 2016. This resource is also available online via a subscription at *www.apstylebook.com.*

The Chicago Manual of Style (16th Edition), The University of Chicago Press, 2010. This resource is also available online via a subscription at *www.chicagomanualofstyle.org.*

Merriam Webster's Collegiate Dictionary, Merriam-Webster Mass Market, 2014. If you're using AP Style, this is your go-to dictionary.

Writer's Digest Desk Grammar Reference, Gary Lutz and Diane Stevenson, WDG, 2005. You can look up any grammar question in this comprehensive reference.

Online Resources

Arrant Pedantry—www.arrantpedantry.com, Jonathon Owen. Jonathon Owen is picky and comforting at the same time.

Captain Grammar Pants—www.facebook.com/Captain-Grammar-Pants -247802875254452, Sean Williams. This amusing Facebook page offers clear explanations for every grammar issue the Captain comes across. Follow her.

Daily Writing Tips—www.dailywritingtips.com, Maeve Maddox, editor. As a general-purpose blog, this website offers tips to a wide range of people who have to write.

Dictionary.com and *Thesaurus.com*. When I write, I keep the tabs open to both these pages so I can flip to them as needed.

Grammar Girl—www.quickanddirtytips.com/grammar-girl, Mignon Fogarty. She's the perfect person to accompany you down grammar rabbit holes. She makes it look easy.

Grammarphobia Blog—www.grammarphobia.com/blog, Patricia T. O'Conner and Stewart Kellerman. A fun and fascinating blog on the world of words.

Useful Writing Courses—www.usefulwritingcourses.com, Carol Tice and Linda Formichelli. The offerings here are varied, with lots of effective tactics and ideas targeted toward striving writers.

Writer's Digest—www.writersdigest.com. Yes, I know, it's the website for aspiring writers. But it's also full of helpful tips for anyone who has to be in the word game. And that's you.

INDEX

ABOUT THE AUTHOR

Mary-Kate Mackey is a teacher, speaker, and writer. After 14 years of honing her signature teaching tools and techniques at the University of Oregon's School of Journalism and Communication, she now leads popular writing workshops at conferences across the United States. An award-winning writer, she co-authored *Sunset's Secret Gardens* and contributed to *Gardening in the Northwest* and the *Sunset Western Garden Book*. Her byline has appeared in numerous national publications including *Fine Gardening, Horticulture*, and *Sunset*.

Find out more at *www.MaryKateMackey.com*.